God Is Addicted To Worship, And I Am His Supplier

(WHY YOUR WORSHIP ISN'T WORKING!)

KENNETH T. WHALUM, JR.

#WorshipWorks

Trilogy Christian Publishers
A Wholly Owned Subsidary of Trinity Broadcasting Network
2442 Michelle Drive
Tustin, CA 92780

Cover design by: Cornerstone Creative Solutions

For information, address Trilogy Christian Publishing
Rights Department, 2442 Michelle Drive, Tustin, Ca 92780.
Trilogy Christian Publishing/ TBN and colophon are trademarks of Trinity Broadcasting Network.

For information about special discounts for bulk purchases, please contact Trilogy Christian Publishing.

Manufactured in the United States of America

10 9 8 7 6 5 4 3 2 1

Library of Congress Cataloging-in-Publication Data is available.

ISBN 978-1-63769-496-1 (Print Book)
ISBN 978-1-63769-497-8 (ebook)

CONTENTS

FOREWORD

————— ⋄○⚮○⋄ —————

While teaching a course at Memphis Theological Seminary, I had the opportunity to engage Pastor Kenneth T. Whalum, Jr. in class. His rigorous intellect, high energy, and ministerial focus was apparent, but it was not until I visited the congregation that he pastors—The New Olivet Worship Center (TNOWC)—that I understood how central worship is in his thought and practice.

I decided to join TNOWC and began participating in The Plan: attendance/participation Sunday morning, Sunday evening, and Wednesday evening. Before each service, I joined Pastor Whalum, ministerial staff, and congregation, worshiping at the altar. Then, I found myself coming to the altar during the work week, as my schedule allowed. Often, I found members of church staff, other congregants, or their children, already there worshiping. Today, the worship life Pastor Whalum has developed through critical and careful examinations of sacred texts continues to inform my life of faith in my work as Associate Pastor at First Baptist Church of Heth, Arkansas.

In his first book, *Hip-Hop is Not Our Enemy*,[1] Pastor Whalum examined aspects of Jesus' cultural location and experience, highlighting parallels within the Hip-Hop community; he challenged those holding an a priori negative perspective on African-American youth's cultural expressions, but who take no responsibility for their own part in shaping moral perspectives. Written with clarity and insight, *God Is Addicted To Worship, And I Am His Supplier* provokes those who claim faith in Jesus to adhere to models of worship set forth in the Bible; every believer is challenged to grow spiritually through worship.

> *"Worship is the most under-developed, under-researched, and unappreciated biblical concept in all of Christendom."*

THE PROPHECY

[Apostle John Eckhardt is overseer of Crusaders Ministries, located in Chicago, Illinois. Gifted with a strong apostolic call, Apostle Eckhardt has ministered throughout the United States and overseas in more than 70 nations. He is a sought-after international conference speaker, has authored more than 20 books, and produces a daily radio broadcast. Of interest to me and the members of our church is his book, *Prayers That Rout Demons and Break Curses.* I use the book as sacred text and teaching material in our weekly Sunday night Worship services, and I am wholly impressed with his intellect and the spiritual soundness of his doctrine. On the fourth Sunday in March of the year 2018, we welcomed him as keynote speaker as part of our annual Men's Month Worship services. The following is a verbatim account of the prophecy he spoke into my life and the life of The New Olivet Worship Center.]

   "The LORD says, 'Son, I've given you an unusual vision, an unusual people.' And the LORD said, 'Get ready, I'm gonna even increase in this House, even My glory and My presence. I'm gonna take you to another level of ministry in raising, and training, and mobilizing my people in this hour to understand even true Worship and what it is to be a Worshiper.' And the LORD said, 'I'm gonna use you to break people free from tra-

dition, and religion. and the things that have held them back from my presence.' And the LORD said, 'Son, it's a new day and new season, in which I'm raising up new voices and new men who have vision for my people.' And the LORD said, 'Even as you continue, my grace is upon your life to raise up not only this generation, but even generations to come.' And the LORD said, 'Son, get ready to write. I'm putting the pen in your hand to write down the things I've given you to write that my people may read it concerning what I'm doing in this House,' says the LORD. And the LORD said, 'It'll not be a hidden thing.' The LORD said, 'I'm going to expose even the vision of this House. I'm going to begin to show others what I'm doing in this place. You'll not be a hidden jewel, but I'm gonna cause my glory to be released from this place into different places where people will begin to drink from the water that flows from this House and the rivers that flow from this House. And out of your belly will flow rivers, and rivers, and rivers, and rivers of living water to bring life, to bring refreshing, to bring liberty, to bring joy, to bring breakthrough in the lives of people. 'So, get ready,' says God. 'I'm putting a new mantle, a new authority, a new unction on your life.' And the LORD said, 'You will not die, but you will live to declare the work of the LORD. You will live. My strength and my grace shall be upon you for years to come,' said the LORD. 'And I'll renew your youth like the eagle. I'll renew your youth like the eagle. And you'll soar high, and you'll lift others up. So, get ready.' I release the word of the LORD in your life. Come on; if you believe it, put those hands together, and thank God for blessing: blessing, favor, miracles, breakthrough, unction in your life. In the name of Jesus, Amen."

[I wrote two books before I wrote *God Is Addicted to Worship, And I Am His Supplier*. One is a very short treatment of the spiritual discipline of fasting, entitled *FASTING: It's Not for Everybody, But It Might Be for You*.[2] The other is entitled, *Hip-Hop Is Not Our Enemy: From A Preacher Who Keeps It Real.* Since my days in seminary, I have felt that there was a shortage of scholastic and/or academic material on Worship, but it was Apostle Eckhardt's prophecy that motivated me to follow through, and I am eternally grateful for his obedience to the Holy Spirit's promptings concerning me and the "Olives" of The New Olivet. It is my prayer that upon reading this book you will be grateful for Apostle Eckhardt's prophecy as well.]

CHAPTER ONE

—◦◦◦◦◦—

How Dare You?

God Is Addicted to Worship, And I Am His Supplier (Why Your Worship Isn't Working!). I hear you Mr. and Ms. Reader: "How dare you use such crass language in reference to God? How could you even fix your mouth to connect the word addicted as an adjective describing God?" The statement itself reveals certain things about the author, of course. As I write this book, I am fully aware of the fact that terms like "addict" and "supplier" (or the much more *urban* terms: "junkie" and "pusher man")—in addition to having strictly pejorative connotations—have long since ceased to be the politically correct descriptions generally in the English lexicon. I choose to revive and highlight them because of the very specific audiences I'm targeting—the AARP (American Association of Retired Persons) crowd—those readers fifty-five years of age and older, also known as Baby Boomers. They (we) did and do use and understand those distasteful terms. As elders we're also the only group of people who have the experience, ability, and authority to correct the dangerous spiritual trajectory America is on. Clearly the clock is ticking on our opportunity to make a positive impact. More specifically, my target audience is *Christian* Baby Boomers. In other words, if you consider yourself saved, having confessed a hope in Christ (probably at an early age) and accepted Him as your personal savior, I'm talking to you. If you're younger than us Baby Boomers, it's my pleasure to let you in on our conversation! My purpose in writing this book is to enlist your help in getting God to heal our land, the United States of America. If you're a Christian who doesn't agree that America is sick and in need of healing, you haven't been paying attention! Before I go any further let me apologize to you if you were offended by this book's title. All I ask is that you keep reading long enough to understand my heart. Hopefully you will see that it is not my intention to offend.

With that said, a definition of terms is in order at this point. What do I mean by the word *addict?* An addict is someone who is physically and mentally dependent on a particular substance and unable to stop taking it without incurring adverse effects; a person who gets an unusual amount of pleasure from or has an unusual amount of interest in something; someone who wants to have or do something all the time; an enthusiastic devotee of a specified thing or activity; a person with a compulsive habit or excessive dependency on, and addiction to a specific substance.[3] A *supplier*, or *pusher man*, is a person who readily produces, promotes, and provides the substance to which the addict or junkie is addicted.[4] GOD IS ADDICTED TO WORSHIP, AND I AM HIS SUPPLIER.

I'll provide additional definitions over the course of the next few pages, but first you and I need to stop somewhere and get a *drink*...of water! Let's see, what about that watering hole in the Samaritan town of Sychar? You know the spot I'm talking about. Some people refer to it as Jacob's well.

Fortunately for us, two very important people are already there. Let's eavesdrop:

John 4:4-26 (New International Version)

4   *Now he had to go through Samaria.*

5   *So he came to a town in Samaria called Sychar, near the plot of ground Jacob had given to his son Joseph.*

6   *Jacob's well was there, and Jesus, tired as he was from the journey, sat down by the well. It was about noon.*

7   *When a Samaritan woman came to draw water, Jesus said to her, Will you give me a drink?*

8   *His disciples had gone into the town to buy food.*

9   *The Samaritan woman said to him, "You are a Jew and I am a Samaritan woman. How can you ask me for a drink?" (For Jews do not associate with Samaritans.)*

10 *Jesus answered her, If you knew the gift of God and who it is that asks you for a drink, you would have asked him, and he would have given you living water.*

11 *"Sir", the woman said, "you have nothing to draw with, and the well is deep. Where can you get this living water?*

12 *Are you greater than our father Jacob; who gave us this well and drank from it himself, as did also his sons and his livestock?"*

13 *Jesus answered, Everyone who drinks this water will be thirsty again,*

14 *but whoever drinks the water that I give them will never thirst. Indeed, the water I give them will become in them a spring of water welling up to eternal life.*

15 *The woman said to him, "Sir, give me this water so that I won't get thirsty and have to keep coming here to draw water."*

16 He told her, Go, call your husband and come back.

17 "I have no husband", she replied. Jesus said to her, You are right when you say you have no husband.

18 The fact is, you have had five husbands, and the man you now have is not your husband. What you have just said is quite true.

19 "Sir", the woman said, "I can see that you are a prophet.

20 Our ancestors worshiped on this mountain, but you Jews claim that the place where we must worship is in Jerusalem."

21 Woman, Jesus replied, believe me, a time is coming when you will worship the Father neither on this mountain nor in Jerusalem.

22 You Samaritans worship what you do not know; we worship what we do know, for salvation is from the Jews.

23 Yet a time is coming and has now come when the true worshipers will worship the Father in the Spirit and in truth, for they are the kind of worshipers the Father seeks.

24 God is spirit, and his worshipers must worship in the Spirit and in truth.

25 The woman said, "I know that Messiah (called Christ) is coming. When he comes, he will explain everything to us."

26 Then Jesus declared, I, the one speaking to you, am he.

You have probably heard or read this story before. In fact, you have probably heard or read it many times. You may have even taught or *preached* it many times. For this story lends itself to the kind of colorful, exciting, and imaginative storytelling that has proven to be extremely effective in highlighting the evangelistic nature of the church universal, or body of Christ. The woman at the well is known, not by her name, but by her location at a moment in time. Her encounter with Christ is a seminal episode in world history, or *His* story. Or, to be more precise, HER story. Her story dovetails with His story in history to make up *our* story. Why? Because of a single word that begins with the letter "w". You see, the story of the woman at the well is not about the *w*oman, or the *w*ell, or the *w*ater in the *w*ell. The story of the woman at the well is about Worship. The word Worship is mentioned ten times in the five verses spanning verse 20 to verse 24. Worship is the most under-developed, under-researched, and unappreciated biblical concept in all of Christendom. I think I'll say that again.

> *"Worship is the most under-developed, under-researched, and unappreciated biblical concept in all of Christendom."*

Let me ask you a question. Something happens at your church every Sunday morning, traditionally at eleven o'clock (although early morning services are increasingly popular these days). What do we call that *something* that happens at the eleven o'clock a.m. hour? We call it Worship. I say we *call* it Worship because the fact of the matter is that very few churches engage in what the marquee in front of the church advertises. It is, in a sense, false advertising. Essentially this book is a clarion call for truth in advertising! If Christian churches call themselves houses or places of Worship— and they do—then they ought to be just that. Not only do most Christian churches call themselves houses or places of Worship, but they aggressively invite others to come and do it with them. Look at this sampling of church marquees in my hometown of Memphis, and you'll see what I'm talking about. *Please understand me*: <u>I am *not* saying that the members of these churches do not Worship</u>. I truly hope they are! I am merely pointing out that a whole lot of churches use the word "Worship" on their church marquees! I have no doubt the same is true in your city.

Of all the activities we engage in as churchgoing Christians there is only one activity that our heavenly Father is truly seeking *if* we believe Jesus' statement in John 4:23. That activity is Worship. (Allow me a brief aside here. Reread the first sentence of this paragraph. I ended that sentence with the clause, "...*if* we believe Jesus' statement in John 4:23." There are some people who instinctively react to that clause with this thought: "*If* we are to believe??? How *dare* you suggest that I don't believe the words of Jesus! And you call yourself a preacher!" Calm down, reader. Think about the import of this. Just because people are Christians does not automatically mean they believe the Word of God, despite their protestations to the contrary. Belief systems precipitate action, and if my actions aren't determined by my professed beliefs, then I don't really believe what I say I believe.) Again, *if* we believe what Jesus told the woman at the well, then we believe that our Father God is *seeking* true Worshipers. We'll need to flesh out some definitional nuances concerning the words "seeking" and "Worship" eventually. But for now, let's stay in shallow water—in the wading pool, if you will. Take a minute right now to run a quick reference in your Bible concordance (King James Version) on the phrase used in that verse, "...the Father seeketh such...". I guarantee you that there is no other biblical text where that statement is made. Let me say it again: If we believe the words of Jesus, there is only one activity that our Father God is seeking. That activity is Worship.

But He isn't seeking Worship in an abstract sense. He's seeking it as an existential imperative, not as a volitional option. Look at John 4:24 again. God is spirit: and they that worship him *must* worship him in spirit and in truth. *If* you're going to Worship him, you *must* Worship him in spirit *and* in truth. And if it's possible to Worship God in truth, then it is also possible to Worship Him in *un*truth, or falsity, and it is possible to Worship Him incorrectly, or insincerely. I hope you are beginning to get a sense of the importance of having a crystal-clear understanding of just what Worship is. Even before we dive deeper into exact definitions, it should be obvious to you that Worship, at least in the eyes of God, is not just an ethereal essence or a mere grammatical construct. It's a layered, substantive, multi-faceted physical, mental, *and* spiritual construct. Additionally, and more importantly, Worship is an action. And it's an action being sought by God right now, this very minute. Nothing has happened in world history since those words were uttered by Jesus to the Samaritan woman at Jacob's well to change their meaning, focus, or thrust. More importantly, Jesus himself never contradicted his statement. In other words, God is *still* seeking true Worshipers, which means He is still seeking true Worship. I don't know about you, but I strive to be a true Worshiper of the God who created me in my mother's womb. I've said it before, and I'll say it again throughout this book:

"Worship is the most under-developed, under-researched, and unappreciated biblical concept in all of Christendom."

Most Christians assume they know what Worship is, and they don't take kindly to questions that challenge their assumptions. They simply ignore those questions. It's time we stopped ignoring the questions.

If Jesus admonishes us to Worship the Father in truth, it is obvious that it is possible to Worship in the opposite of truth. The opposite of truth is dishonesty or falsity. It stands to reason then that any form of Worship that does not comport with what Jesus meant is dishonest or false Worship. Take a deep breath, because I know what I just said may offend traditional religious sensibilities. Before we get into the definitions that are so crucial to an understanding of Worship, please allow me to challenge you to test my hypothesis concerning your own views and the views of people whose opinions you respect. It may even give you appreciable insight into the subtitle of this book: (Why Your Worship Isn't Working!) I'm providing two empty spaces below, each of which is preceded by a simple question. Please write your answer to the first question in the space provided and write a friend's answer in the other. Then we'll proceed! (Caveat: Please write in pencil, just in case you change your mind after you read this book!)

1. What is your definition of Worship?

   _____

   _____

2. Choose a friend whose opinions you respect, and ask them, "What is your definition of Worship?" (Please write their answer in the space provided.)

   _____

   _____

We'll get to the definitions soon, but there's something we'll have to deal with first, and it's in the next chapter.

CHAPTER TWO

Before We Can Talk About What Worship Is, We Must Talk About What It's Not!

You have noticed by now that when I use the word Worship I capitalize it. I realize this practice is contrary to literary and grammatical convention. In fact, it's grammatically incorrect; I don't care. Worship is so transformational, and so important, and so vital to our existence and future that I am intentionally elevating it to capital status. Before we can talk about what Worship is, we must talk about what it's not. Worship is not praise. Worship is not music. Worship is not dancing. Worship is not preaching. Worship is not praying. Let me explain.

Worship Is Not Praise

Worship is not praise. Have you ever noticed how many times, especially in church circles, you hear the terms Worship and praise used interchangeably? And often they're used in connection with some form of music ministry, as though they denote a style, genre, format, or rhythmic arrangement of music. What is most disconcerting to me is that church leaders, specifically Pastors and ministers of music them-selves, use the terms interchangeably, with no apparent inter-est in the biblical difference and distinction between the two. I'll get into the music portion of this discussion later but suffice it to say that the music ministry of the church will be much more effective when and if church leaders accept the fact that Worship and praise are not the same thing. Worship is not praise. The word praise as it is used in the Bible literally means to "flash forth light" on God by being boastful about Him.[5]

Praise is expression, usually verbal, of approval or com-mendation.[6] Praise is not Worship. Praise is praise. Worship is Worship. To be sure, if we Worship God aright, we can't help but be led to praise Him for His wondrous works. If we Worship God aright, we submit ourselves to God as being so much greater than we are, and then we think about the fact that even though He's so much bigger and so much greater He gives us second chances to get life right by showing love in the way He commands. Reflexively, upon that realization, we want to praise Him. But again, Worship is not praise. Think about it; if Worship and praise are synonymous, would God have inspired scripture to be written as though they were not? I mean, come on!

Worship Is Not Music

Worship is not music. To be sure, music is *conducive* to Worship. Music can enhance Worship. Music can set the atmosphere for Worship, and even change the atmosphere during Worship. But music is not Worship, and Worship is not music. Music is music, and Worship is Worship. This attempted fusion—perhaps even unconsciously so—of two totally distinct terms is the reason most church-going Christians are confused and/or uneducated about Worship. No, confused isn't really the word I want to use, although it applies. The more accurate and appropriate adjective is *ignorant*. I don't mean that in a pejorative sense. It's just that the people of God are functionally and literally ignorant of the meaning of Worship, which is even more shocking when one considers that Worship is the object of God's one continual craving. He's experiencing that craving even now, two millennia after Jesus gave the revelation to that woman at that well. Music is so important to the Worship experience that it's a shame that so few music leaders are aware of what Worship really is. I can't stress it enough; music is ***soooooo*** important, impactful, and imperative in relation to the Worship experience! Music is important, impactful, and imperative, PERIOD! Music evokes mental, spiritual, and physical responses. Think about your favorite songs. When you hear them on the radio or on your smart device, they evoke sometimes visceral responses. A lively song makes you want to dance. A sad song makes you want to contemplate. A slow, sensual song makes you want to slow dance. I've even heard people say that their babies were conceived to a particular song, because love music made them want to make love. Well, Worship music ought to make you want to Worship!

I asked two professional music ministers the following question: "Why do you think so many Christians, especially preachers and ministers of music, use the terms praise and Worship interchangeably?" These two professional music ministers are both my respected friends. One is Grammy-award winning artist, songwriter, and producer Donald Lawrence. His answer to my question was, "Because they also use 'Took my feet out of the miry clay and placed them on a rock to stay,' and 'You don't know like I know what the Lord has done for me,' and 'When I think of His goodness and all He's done for me…'. The reason preachers and ministers of music continue to use the terms praise and Worship interchangeably is lack of revelation." The other professional music minister I asked is songwriter, arranger, producer, vocalist, and New Olivet Worship Center Music Ministry Director Dr. Allen Todd, PhD. His answer was, "I think Christians, especially preachers and ministers of music, have heard and have taught the phrase 'praise and Worship' as one action for so long that it is programmed in their minds as one. Now it has become doctrine in our churches, which makes it difficult to accept, think, practice and/or engage in them separately. I suppose vain tradition makes it easier to keep them as one." Think about that last sentence for a minute: "Vain tradition makes it easier to keep them as one." Even though a simple dictionary inquiry—not to mention a biblical concordance review—makes clear that praise and Worship are not the same thing, man's vain tradition is strong enough to cause Christians to ignore the distinction.

That's not just the opinion of Donald Lawrence, Dr. Allen Todd, and me. It's an opinion that is grounded in the opinion of Jesus Christ. Let's look at Mark 7:1-8 (KJV):

1   *Then came together unto him the Pharisees, and certain of the scribes, which came from Jerusalem.*

2   *And when they saw some of his disciples eat bread with defiled, that is to say, with unwashen, hands, they found fault.*

3   *For the Pharisees, and all the Jews, except they wash their hands oft, eat not, holding the tradition of the elders.*

4   *And when they come from the market, except they wash, they eat not. And many other things there be, which they have received to hold, as the washing of cups, and pots, brasen vessels, and of tables.*

5   *Then the Pharisees and scribes asked him, Why walk not thy disciples according to the tradition of the elders, but eat bread with unwashen hands?*

6   *He answered and said unto them, Well hath Esaias prophesied of you hypocrites, as it is written, This people honoureth me with their lips, but their heart is far from me.*

7   *Howbeit in vain do they worship me, teaching for doctrines the commandments of men.*

8   *For laying aside the commandment of God, ye hold the tradition of men, as the washing of pots and cups: and many other such like things ye do.*

The refusal of Pastors and ministers of music to even acknowledge that Worship and music are not synonymous may be the single most prevalent reason why so many Christians are in complete darkness concerning the one thing our Father God craves. Donald Lawrence is right. We get so used to doing things a certain way that we start to turn a blind eye and a deaf ear to anything that challenges the presuppositions and preferences we've collectively established through centuries of practice. Anyone who has ever tried to implement anything new in church has heard the retort: "No, we can't do it your way because we've always done it like we're doing it now." Music is not Worship. Worship is not music. Music is music. Worship is Worship. If you think music is Worship, prove it!

I included the comparisons between Worship, praise, and music because those are the three areas that Christians tend to confuse and conflate in their understanding, or lack thereof, of Worship. These next three I am including because of their collective ubiquity in the church-going experience of most Christians, particularly Black Christians. When Black Christians are asked to reflect on their collective Sunday Worship experience, they tend to combine the three previous elements, Worship, praise, and music, with the following three elements: dancing, preaching, and praying. This is typically what most people think of when they think of Sunday Worship "services."

Worship Is Not Dancing

Worship is not dancing. To dance is to move the feet and body to rhythm. Dancing is not Worship. Dancing is dancing. Worship is Worship. Dancing is very closely connected to praise. In fact, Psalm 150:4 is a literal *command* to "praise him (the LORD) *with* the timbrel *and* dance." Dancing is a dicey subject among church folks. Most traditional Christians frown on any form of dance. In recent years, "praise dancers" have been added to the liturgical sequence in many churches, but in this context the dancing is extremely conservative and choreographed to be more hand movement and "beginners" ballet, if you will, than full-on dancing. In the African-American church community dancing has a different connotation altogether, particularly in so-called Pentecostal denominations like Church Of God In Christ (C.O.G.I.C.). Many Black Baptist churches also practice the form of dance I'm about to describe. It's called the "holy dance." It is a beautiful, rhythmic (*always* fast-moving), passionate, intensely personal expression of joy and release in the Spirit. It's an ecstatic state that is brought on by a combination of music, singing, lyrical content, and reflection on the goodness of God. It is called holy dancing because it bears very little resemblance to the dancing that might be done in a night club or at a college party, which tends more toward structure and often, quite frankly, sexual overtones.

Early in my pastoring ministry, I faced significant backlash from older congregants who objected vociferously to my penchant for unconventional dancing in church, and the fact that I encouraged young people to come to the altar and dance with me. My detractors would say, "The only kind of dancing that should be done in church is the holy dance." That bothered me, because I truly did not want to offend the older church members who loved me, and whom I loved. So, I researched the term "holy dance" in the Bible. What I found was that that term is not used in scripture, although there are countless instances of dancing. My favorite example is David's dancing in 2 Samuel 6:12-16 (NIV) as follows:

> *12 Now King David was told, "The LORD has blessed the household of Obed-Edom and everything he has, because of the ark of God." So David went to bring up*

the ark of God from the house of Obed-Edom to the
City of David with rejoicing.
13 When those who were carrying the ark of the LORD
had taken six steps, he sacrificed a bull and a fattened
calf.
14 Wearing a linen ephod, David was dancing before the
LORD with all his might,
15 while he and all Israel were bringing up the ark of the
LORD with shouts and the sound of trumpets.
16 As the ark of the LORD was entering the City of
David, Michal daughter of Saul watched from a
window. And when she saw King David leaping and
dancing before the LORD, she despised him in her
heart.

No, there is no such thing as a holy dance in the Bible, but it cannot be disputed that King David was a holy dancer! Interestingly, when David's wife Michal saw David expressing his joy through dancing, she "hated" him. Now is not the time to discuss the effects of envy and jealousy on church protocol but suffice it to say that "haters" still exist in the church today. But again, dancing is not Worship. Dancing is dancing. Worship is Worship. If you think dancing, even holy dancing if you still think there is such a thing, is Worship, prove it!

Worship Is Not Preaching

Worship is not preaching. To preach is to announce, declare, proclaim the gospel of Jesus Christ. Preaching is not Worship. Preaching is preaching. Worship is Worship. If you think preaching is Worship, prove it!

Worship Is Not Praying

Worship is not praying. To pray is to speak to God, letting your requests be made known to Him. But prayer is not Worship. Worship is not prayer. Prayer is prayer. Worship is Worship. If you think prayer is Worship, prove it!

So, for the sake of review:

Worship Is <u>Not</u> Praise
Worship Is <u>Not</u> Music
Worship Is <u>Not</u> Dancing
Worship Is <u>Not</u> Preaching
Worship Is <u>Not</u> Praying

If your reaction to these distinctions is, "It's not that big a deal," despite the implication of Jesus' statement to the contrary, you are suggesting (perhaps subconsciously) that Jesus himself did not know the difference between Worship, praise, music, dancing, preaching, and praying. If Jesus had meant to say praise, he would have said praise. If he had meant to say music, he would have said music. If he had meant to say dancing, he would have said dancing. If he had meant to say preaching, he would have said preaching. If he had meant to say praying, he would have said praying. But he didn't use either of those terms. He used the term, *Worship*. Before reading further, it would probably be helpful to you to review what you've read so far. Why? Because I guarantee that your own doubt, as well as pushback from other Christians who are steeped in their religious tradition, will cause you to question this new understanding and clarity regarding Worship. The concepts I flesh out in this book are biblical, doctrinally sound, and theologically pure. Purity of substance is very important to an addict. Every addict wants his or her cocaine or heroin or *whatever* undiluted and in its purest form. God is an addict, and I am His supplier.

A great deal of the credit, and/or responsibility, and/or blame for what the Body of Christ knows or doesn't know about Worship belongs to the Christian preachers and teachers we follow. There are, of course, countless men and women who have occupied pulpits across the centuries, and it is impossible to name them all. I think, however, that a sampling of two or three respected preachers of my generation will prove my point. The reason Christians generally have no idea what the difference between Worship and praise is (and the other practices that I have listed in this chapter) is because many Christian preachers have not yet received the full revelation themselves. One such respected preacher was Dr. Myles Munroe, founder, president, and senior Pastor of Bahamas Faith Ministries International, headquartered in Nassau, Bahamas.[7] In his book, *The Purpose and Power of Love & Marriage*, Dr. Munroe discusses the importance of Worship to the life of a Christian, particularly in the context of marriage, as a means of practicing and demonstrating our love for God. The following paragraph is an extensive, but illustrative, example of an incomplete understanding of what true Worship is. I have italicized those portions of Dr. Munroe's assertions that further highlight the need for the book you're reading right now, although I wholeheartedly agree with much of what he says otherwise.

> At this point it is important to understand that much of what we often call worship is really something else. *True worship occurs on a spiritual rather than a physical plane.* So much of our so-called worship takes place on the physical level:

Singing, praying, lifting hands, dancing, speaking in tongues, etc. While these activities engage the body and the mind, they do not necessarily or automatically engage the spirit. We can do all those things with great fervor and energy, and yet never enter into genuine worship. What most believers call worship is in reality praise. To praise God means to lift Him up, to speak well of Him, to hold Him in highest esteem, to ascribe to Him glory and majesty and honor. All of these things are good and proper and appropriate—but they are not true worship. Praise prepares the way for worship, but that's as far as many believers ever go. *True worship always occurs spirit to Spirit*—our spirit mingling with the Spirit of God. More often than not, it takes place without words. The word worship means to interface or interact with, to bow down, to kiss. In short, worship means intimacy. That is what sets worship apart from praise. There is no such thing as long-distance intimacy. We can praise God from a distance, but we cannot worship Him from a distance. *Praise is physical; worship is spiritual. Worship is an exchange of selves.*[8]

As I said, I agree with much of what Dr. Munroe says. It is important, however, to clarify where I disagree with the italicized statements:

*"True worship occurs on a spiritual
rather than a physical plane."*

Actually, true Worship occurs on a spiritual *and* a physical plane. The two (spiritual and physical) are not mutually exclusive when it comes to Worship. Jesus must have had this in mind when he clearly established God's expectation for our Worship, which is that we Worship Him "in spirit and in truth" (John 4:24, KJV).

"True worship always occurs spirit to Spirit..."

Again, the two are not mutually exclusive, neither can they be as long as human beings are spirit beings housed in a physical body. True Worship must occur in spirit and in the physical if it is to be pleasing to God.

*"Praise is physical; worship is spiritual.
Worship is an exchange of selves."*

I lift this passage not just to reinforce my opinion that spiritual and physical Worship are not mutually exclusive, but to simply suggest that part of the reason Christians are not clear on what Worship is, is because of preachers' penchant for ethereal language that really doesn't say much of anything substantive, but sounds really pretty!

*"Worship is the most under-developed, under-researched,
and unappreciated biblical concept in all of Christendom."*

CHAPTER THREE

---∞✦∞---

What Is Worship?

An addict, or junkie, is a person who is dependent upon a particular substance. In case you haven't figured it out by now, I'm a wordsmith, and I believe words mean something. The word substance means the most important or essential part of something. According to Jesus, there is no more important or essential part of our relationship with God than our Worship. Every junkie wants his or her crack cocaine or heroin or opioids, or whatever their addictive substance of choice is, undiluted and in its purest form. I can see your eyebrows arching in incredulity as you read that sentence, so let me hurry and provide those definitions I promised! What is Worship? What, exactly, was Jesus referring to when he told the Samaritan woman that "the Father *seeketh*" true Worshippers? We'll unpack that word "seeketh" shortly, but for now let's zero in on Worship. What was Jesus talking about when he used that word in John 4:23 (KJV)? Here's the verse again:

But the hour cometh, and now is, when the true
worshippers shall worship the Father in spirit and in
truth: for the Father seeketh such to worship him.

The word Worship is derived from the Greek translation of the original Hebrew text.[9] The Greek word for Worship is ***proskuneo,*** and it means:

1. To kiss the hand towards one (in other words, to blow a kiss), in token of reverence
2. To fall upon the knees and touch the ground with the forehead as an expression of profound reverence
3. By kneeling or prostration to do homage or make obeisance.[10]

Now, if you're anything like I was before I received the revelation on Worship and studied the scriptures on it, you need to unpack the definition a bit more, because words like reverence, prostration, homage, and obeisance are not found floating effortlessly around in our casual conversations with family and friends these days. Let's take the time to flesh out and grasp as much meaning as we can:

1. The word *reverence* means "deep respect for some-one or something; a gesture indicative of respect; a bow or curtsy".[11]
2. The word *prostration* means "the action of lying stretched out face down on the ground".[12]
3. The word *homage* means "special honor or respect shown publicly".[13]
4. The word *obeisance* means "a gesture or *movement of the body* that expresses deference".[14]

5. The word *deference* means "humble submission and respect".[15]
6. The word *humble* means "having or *showing* a modest or low estimate of one's own importance." It means "to lower *oneself*".[16] This word *humble* is very important to a complete understanding of Worship. Look at the Hebrew definition: "To be *brought down*; to *be* under; to *be* low.[17]

It is clear, then, that Worship is a physical act. Let me say that again: TRUE WORSHIP IS A PHYSICAL ACT. Worship is not some abstract, ideological, theological construct with vague references to humility, and spiritual lifestyles, and states of mind. It is equally clear from the layered definition of the word, that the physical act entails bowing, and/or kneeling, and/or "blowing kisses," and/or laying prostrate. Remember that when you get to church Sunday! With that said, I have a feeling you're not completely convinced that Worship is a physical act.

Consider the following biblical examples:

*   2 Chronicles 20:18, *Jehoshaphat bowed down with his face to the ground, and all the people of Judah and Jerusalem fell down in worship before the LORD* (NIV).
*   Daniel 3:7, *Therefore, as soon as they heard the sound of the horn, flute, zither, lyre, harp and all kinds of music, all the nations and peoples of every language fell down and worshiped the image of gold that King Nebuchadnezzar had set up* (NIV).
*   Job 1:20 (KJV).
*   Matthew 2:11, *And when they were come into the house, they saw the young child with Mary his mother,*

and fell down, and worshipped him: and when they had opened their treasures, they presented unto him gifts; gold, and frankincense, and myrrh (KJV).
- Matthew 4:8,9, *Again, the devil taketh him up into an exceeding high mountain, and sheweth him all the kingdoms of the world, and the glory of them; And saith unto him, All these things will I give thee, if thou wilt fall down and worship me* (KJV).
- There are other biblical examples. Lots of others. I have a feeling you know that intuitively already. But just in case you don't, please take some time right now to search the scriptures yourself. You'll find that almost every time you read the word *Worship* in scripture it's in connection with somebody bowing, kneeling, or laying prostrate.

Let's go deeper. There's another word in that Johannine passage that sheds additional indispensable light on what Jesus meant by his references to Worship. He says God is *seeking* true Worshipers. The exact word in the King James Version is *seeketh*. Seeketh in Greek is *dzeteo*, and it means to feel a powerful desire for; to seek in order to find out by thinking, meditating, reasoning; to inquire into; to strive after; to crave.[18]

Of all the activities that we engage in as churchgoing Christians, there is only one activity that God is truly seeking or craving. God the Father is thinking on Worship this very minute! He's meditating, and reasoning, and inquiring into our lives, and into our families, and into our churches, trying to find some Worship to satisfy His craving. Please try to receive and absorb this into your spirit. God is going to great lengths to get from us the thing He's seeking. And that thing is Worship. But that's not all. God isn't just thinking on

Worship. God is striving for Worship. You know how we work hard on our jobs or in our businesses because we're striving to make a living? You know how we study hard and prepare for tests because we want to do well in school? You know how we pursue romantic relationships with people because we're striving to be happy? You know how we want to earn more money because we're striving to buy more things? God has that same mindset when it comes to Worship. He's striving for it. He craves it. God cannot be comfortable unless and until He gets some Worship.

Worship is an important and critical part of the church's arsenal of spiritual weaponry. That's the reason our adversary the devil has blinded our eyes to it. Satan doesn't mind you going to church. He just doesn't want you Worshiping God while you're there, or anywhere else, for that matter. Let me warn you, by the time you finish reading this book, you're going to be responsible for acting on the knowledge you've gained from reading it. Think about it. How can we call ourselves Christians, and call our churches houses of Worship, yet not actually engage in Worship? How could we not give God what God craves? God literally craves your Worship. A craving is a strong need or compulsion that will not stop until it is satisfied. Addicts develop cravings for whatever substance or activity they're addicted to. Drug addicts are known to have physical reactions to cravings. It's called "jonesing."[19] Pregnant women often describe peculiar cravings during the term of their pregnancy. My wife Sheila has blessed me with three sons. Each is a grown man now, and each of them stands at least six feet tall, so it's hard to imagine them ever being tiny enough to fit in their mother's womb. But as developing fetuses, they must have had enormous appetites, because Sheila often experienced voracious food cravings before they were born.

One episode, in particular, stands out in my mind. Late one night as we settled in bed, Sheila nudged me and said she was hungry. Not just hungry, mind you, but hungry for a rib sandwich. At the time, we owned and managed a barbeque restaurant called K-Twigg's BBQ & More. The restaurant was very close to our home, so I climbed out of bed, put my clothes on, and drove to K-Twigg's. I told one of our workers to wrap some ribs in aluminum foil and to give me two slices of bread in wax paper and a small container of coleslaw (It's a Memphis thing!). With a great degree of self-satisfaction for going out of my way to satisfy my pregnant wife's craving, I placed these three items in a plastic bag and returned to our home and my beautiful, pregnant, hungry wife. I handed her the bag, which she eagerly opened while I climbed back into bed. At that moment, when my sweet, pregnant, hungry little wife noticed the ribs and bread wrapped separately, and the cole slaw in a separate container, she handed it all back to me and said, not so sweetly, "I don't want this! I said I wanted a rib *sandwich*, not ribs and bread!" You see, Sheila had a specific craving for a specific thing, and she wasn't going to settle for anything other than or less than that thing.

God is a junkie, and I am His pusher man. God is addicted to Worship, and I am His supplier. The devil is trying to break God's habit. He wants to put God in treatment and force Him to go "cold turkey." As with most familial situations involving addiction, though, Satan is having a problem with his plan. You see, I am a co-dependent enabler of God's addiction to Worship. I supply Him with it every chance I get! I've heard Christians say, "People Worship in different ways. I can Worship any way I want to. There are lots of ways to Worship." Not so. Worship is a physical act. Some may push back against that assertion because they've been conditioned by their own church experience to spiritualize anything and everything connected with God. When asked to define Worship they invariably use vague and nebulous statements that relate somehow to one's state of mind. Their answers typically sound like what you get when you Google the word Worship: "the feeling or expression of reverence and adoration for a deity."[20] Worship is indeed expression! It's your body as the instrument of expression.

Worship is a physical act. Through our Worship, we are saying to God, "Lord, I'm not worthy to stand in your presence. I don't have enough education to make me worthy to stand in your presence. I don't make enough money to make me worthy to stand in your presence." We cannot cavalierly enter God's presence without acknowledging, in some tangible way, that we realize who God is, and that God is our sovereign ruler, and that we are his loyal subjects. Worship is the physical recognition that you are in the presence of royalty, His Majesty. God wants us to respect Him so much that we'll lay out prostrate in His presence, especially at our local churches that we call His house. The Apostle Paul put it this way in Romans 12:1, "I beseech you therefore, brethren, by the mercies of God, that ye present your bodies a living sacrifice, *holy*, acceptable unto God, which is your reasonable service" (KJV).

One of the synonyms for the word holy is pure. Purity of substance is important to a junkie. Every junkie, every addict, wants their "stuff" in its purest form. They want it undiluted. I know I did in my college days when I was on cocaine, marijuana, alcohol, and pills. I wanted mine uncut, because the purer the substance the higher the high—the deeper the satisfaction. In fact, my favorite song during that time in my life was Parliament's "P-Funk":

Make my funk the P. Funk, I want my funk uncut
Make my funk the P. Funk, I wants to get funked up

I want the bomb, I want the P. Funk, I want my funk uncut
Make my funk the P. Funk, I wants to get funked up
Make my funk the P. Funk, I want my funk uncut
Make my funk the P. Funk, I wants to get funked up
I want the bomb, I want the P. Funk,
Don't want my funk stepped on
Make my funk the P. Funk, Before I take it home[21]

P as in pure. It's difficult to feel like giving God pure Worship when our hearts are not pure, but Worship purifies our hearts as we Worship. The Psalmist David must have had this in mind when he penned the following words in Psalm 51:1-10 (KJV):

1   *Have mercy upon me, O God, according to thy loving-kindness: according unto the multitude of thy tender mercies blot out my transgressions.*

2   *Wash me throughly from mine iniquity, and cleanse me from my sin.*

3   *For I acknowledge my transgressions: and my sin is ever before me.*

4   *Against thee, thee only, have I sinned, and done this evil in thy sight: that thou mightest be justified when thou speakest, and be clear when thou judgest.*

5   *Behold, I was shapen in iniquity; and in sin did my mother conceive me.*

6   *Behold, thou desirest truth in the inward parts: and in the hidden part thou shalt make me to know wisdom.*

7   *Purge me with hyssop, and I shall be clean: wash me, and I shall be whiter than snow.*

8   *Make me to hear joy and gladness; that the bones which thou hast broken may rejoice.*

9   Hide thy face from my sins, and blot out all mine iniquities.
10   Create in me a clean heart, O God; and renew a right spirit within me.

David was a Worshiper, and as such he wanted to give God the purest form of his Worship. David, being a man after God's own heart, knew that God craves Worship, like a junkie craves a "fix." In this sense, David was a supplier; one of God's pusher men—as am I—and as I hope you will become. I guess you could say I'm in the pusher recruitment business. And what I'm pushing is the theory that Worship is a physical act that we can supply God with.

"Worship is the most under-developed, under-researched, and unappreciated biblical concept in all of Christendom."

CHAPTER FOUR

Facetime With God

I don't blame you if you are a bit hesitant to buy completely into my theory that Worship is a physical. It just goes against the grain of what most people experience in church settings. If you are a Christian, however, you probably don't have any trouble whatsoever accepting or believing what the Bible says about certain things. This chapter will be devoted to conducting an exhaustive survey of scriptural references to Worship as a physical act. Prostration is the original and most dominant form of Worship. To lie prostrate in this context means to lie on one's face in homage and obeisance to God. I call it spiritual "FaceTime", a term I adapted from the video chat application developed by Apple Computers on June 7, 2010.[22] In the chapter entitled, "What Is Worship" I catalogued five scriptures that clearly describe Worship as a physical act which encompasses falling on one's face. Now, I will share others, because I really do want you to feel comfortable with what is quite possibly a brand new way of looking at Worship for you.

Genesis 17:3, *And Abram fell on his face: and God talked with him, saying,* (KJV)

Numbers 20:6, *Moses and Aaron went from the assembly to the entrance to the tent of meeting and fell facedown, and the glory of the LORD appeared to them* (NIV).

1 Chronicles 29:20, *And David said to all the congregation, Now bless the LORD your God. And all the congregation blessed the LORD God of their fathers, and bowed down their heads, and worshipped the LORD, and the king* (KJV).

1 Kings 1:23, *And they told the king, saying, Behold Nathan the prophet. And when he was come in before the king, he bowed himself before the king with his face to the ground* (KJV).

1 Kings 1:31, *Then Bathsheba bowed down with her face to the ground, prostrating herself before the king, and said, "May my lord King David live forever!"* (NIV)

1 Kings 1:47, *And moreover the king's servants came to bless our lord king David, saying, God make the name of Solomon better than thy name, and make his throne greater than thy throne. And the king bowed himself upon the bed* (KJV).

1 Kings 18:39, *And when all the people saw it, they fell on their faces: and they said, The LORD, he is the God; the LORD, he is the God* (KJV).

Nehemiah 8:6, *And Ezra blessed the LORD, the great God. And all the people answered, Amen, Amen, with lifting up their hands: and they bowed their heads, and worshipped the LORD with their faces to the ground* (KJV).

Ezekiel 1:28, *Like the appearance of a rainbow in the clouds on a rainy day, so was the radiance around him. This was the appearance of the likeness of the glory of the LORD. When I saw it, I fell facedown, and I heard the voice of one speaking* (KJV).

Leviticus 9:24, *And there came a fire out from before the Lord, and consumed upon the altar the burnt offering and the fat: which when all the people saw, they shouted, and fell on their faces* (KJV).

Numbers 16:4, *And when Moses heard it, he fell upon his face:* (KJV)

Numbers 16:22, *And they fell upon their faces, and said, O God, the God of the spirits of all flesh, shall one man sin, and wilt thou be wroth with all the congregation?* (KJV)

Numbers 16:45, *Get you up from among this congregation, that I may consume them as in a moment. And they fell upon their faces* (KJV).

Numbers 22:31, *Then the LORD opened the eyes of Balaam, and he saw the angel of the LORD standing in the way, and his sword drawn in his hand: and he bowed down his head, and fell flat on his face* (KJV).

1 Samuel 24:8, *Then David went out of the cave and called out to Saul, "My lord the king!" When Saul looked behind him, David bowed down and prostrated himself with his face to the ground* (NIV).

1 Samuel 25:23, *When Abigail saw David, she hurried and dismounted from her donkey, and fell on her face before David and bowed herself to the ground* (KJV).

1 Samuel 25:41, *And she arose, and bowed herself on her face to the earth, and said, Behold, let thine handmaid be a servant to wash the feet of the servants of my lord* (KJV).

1 Samuel 28:14, *"What does he look like?" he asked. "An old man wearing a robe is coming up," she said. Then Saul knew it was Samuel, and he bowed down and prostrated himself with his face to the ground* (NIV).

2 Samuel 9:6, *Now when Mephibosheth, the son of Jonathan, the son of Saul, was come unto David, he fell on his*

face, and did reverence. And David said, Mephibosheth. And he answered, Behold thy servant! (KJV)

2 Samuel 9:8, *And he bowed himself, and said, What is thy servant, that thou shouldest look upon such a dead dog as I am?* (KJV)

2 Samuel 14:4, *And when the woman of Tekoah spake to the king, she fell on her face to the ground, and did obeisance, and said, Help, O king* (KJV).

Ruth 2:10, *At this, she bowed down with her face to the ground. She asked him, "Why have I found such favor in your eyes that you notice me—a foreigner?"* (NIV)

Deuteronomy 9:18, *Then once again I fell prostrate before the LORD for forty days and forty nights; I ate no bread and drank no water, because of all the sin you had committed, doing what was evil in the LORD's sight and so arousing his anger* (NIV).

Joshua 5:14, *And he said, Nay; but as captain of the host of the LORD am I now come. And Joshua fell on his face to the earth, and did worship, and said unto him, What saith my lord unto his servant?* (KJV)

Judges 13:20, *For it came to pass, when the flame went up toward heaven from off the altar, that the angel of the LORD ascended in the flame of the altar. And Manoah and his wife looked on it, and fell on their faces to the ground* (KJV).

1 Chronicles 21:16, *David looked up and saw the angel of the LORD standing between heaven and earth, with a drawn sword in his hand extended over Jerusalem. Then David and the elders, clothed in sackcloth, fell facedown* (NIV).

Daniel 2:46, *Then the king Nebuchadnezzar fell upon his face, and worshipped Daniel, and commanded that they should offer an oblation and sweet odours unto him* (KJV).

Daniel 8:17, *So he came near where I stood: and when he came, I was afraid, and fell upon my face: but he said unto me,*

Understand, O son of man: for at the time of the end shall be the vision (KJV).

Joshua 7:6, *And Joshua rent his clothes, and fell to the earth upon his face before the ark of the LORD until the eventide, he and the elders of Israel, and put dust upon their heads* (KJV).

Ezekiel 9:8, *And it came to pass, while they were slaying them, and I was left, that I fell upon my face, and cried, and said, Ah Lord GOD! wilt thou destroy all the residue of Israel in thy pouring out of thy fury upon Jerusalem?* (KJV)

Matthew 17:6, *When the disciples heard this, they fell facedown to the ground, terrified* (NIV).

Matthew 26:39, *And he went a little further, and fell on his face, and prayed, saying, O my Father, if it be possible, let this cup pass from me: nevertheless not as I will, but as thou wilt* (KJV).

Mark 3:11, *And unclean spirits, when they saw him, fell down before him, and cried, saying, Thou art the Son of God* (KJV).

Luke 5:12, *And it came to pass, when he was in a certain city, behold a man full of leprosy: who seeing Jesus fell on his face, and besought him, saying, Lord, if thou wilt, thou canst make me clean* (KJV).

Luke 24:5, *In their fright the women bowed down with their faces to the ground, but the men said to them, "Why do you look for the living among the dead?* (NIV)

Revelation 7:11, *All the angels were standing around the throne and around the elders and the four living creatures. They fell down on their faces before the throne and worshiped God* (NIV).

Revelation 11:16, *And the twenty-four elders, who were seated on their thrones before God, fell on their faces and worshiped God* (NIV).

That's thirty-seven verses, in various translations, clearly describing Worship as a physical act. There are probably more, but if thirty-seven of them won't raise your comfort level about what is obviously the truth, I'm not sure if a few more would do the trick either. I'll leave it at this: Fall on your face and pray about it.

Worship is the most under-developed, under-researched, and unappreciated biblical concept in all of Christendom.

—————◦◦◦◦◦—————

CHAPTER FIVE

Not Everybody Wants God To Have Our Worship

On the other hand, not everybody wants God to receive the Worship He craves, just as not everybody wants the junkie to receive his fix in its purest form. America, especially urban America, is no stranger to this concept. Famous actor Denzel Washington won a Black Entertainment Television (B.E.T.) Award for Best Actor for his portrayal of an infamous Harlem drug dealer named Frank Lucas in the 2007 movie *American Gangster*. Frank Lucas rose to power in corrupt 1970's New York, equaling and eventually surpassing the notorious Mafia crime families with the reach of his illicit empire. His riches and wealth came due to profit from the sale of a pure and potent brand of heroin imported from Saigon, called "Blue Magic." Many people died when one of Lucas' competitors began selling diluted heroin laced with poison and calling it by the same name, "Blue Magic." Similarly, the devil wants us to offer God inauthentic, counterfeit Worship, a cheap imitation. When we don't understand what true Worship is, and when we offer God praise, music, dancing, preaching, and prayer disguised as Worship or misidentified as Worship, we're offering Him counterfeit Worship: inauthentic Worship, fake Worship. That's exactly what the devil wants, because he does not want us to give God the Worship God craves. How do I know Worship is precious to God, and that He craves it like a junkie craves a fix? I'm glad you asked! Because of the lengths to which the devil will go to try to prevent us from Worshiping! Keep reading.

Make no mistake about it, many Christians may be confused about what Worship is, but trust me: the devil is *not*. We know this because of an encounter between Jesus and the devil shortly after John the Baptist baptized Jesus in the Jordan River. Still dripping with water, and immediately upon hearing a voice from heaven say, "This is my beloved Son, in whom I am well pleased," Jesus was, according to Matthew's gospel, led up of the Spirit into the wilderness for one purpose: to be tempted of the devil. And when Jesus had fasted forty days and forty nights, according to the text, he was afterward an hungred (Matthew 4:2, KJV). It was then that Jesus experienced the most intense and ferocious spiritual attack ever launched upon man personally by the devil himself. It was a three-pronged attack. Using a boxing analogy, Jesus and the devil went toe-to-toe for three rounds. The first two rounds are found in Matthew 4:3-7, KJV:

> 3 *And when the tempter came to him, he said, If thou be the Son of God, command that these stones be made bread.*
>
> 4 *But he answered and said, It is written, Man shall not live by bread alone, but by every word that proceedeth out of the mouth of God.*

5   *Then the devil taketh him up into the holy city, and setteth him on a pinnacle of the temple,*

6   *And saith unto him, If thou be the Son of God, cast thyself down: for it is written, He shall give his angels charge concerning thee: and in their hands they shall bear thee up, lest at any time thou dash thy foot against a stone.*

7   *Jesus said unto him, It is written again, Thou shalt not tempt the Lord thy God.*

Clearly, Jesus was prepared for these jabs from his opponent, as indicated by his crisp verbal counterpunching. But the devil had one last punch he wanted to throw. Let's call it a "haymaker" which, if it landed, would have changed the course of history. He got down to the nitty gritty, revealing what he wanted most from Jesus in Matthew 4:8-11, KJV. Let's listen in:

8   *Again, the devil taketh him up into an exceeding high mountain, and sheweth him all the kingdoms of the world, and the glory of them;*

9   *And saith unto him, All these things will I give thee, if thou wilt fall down and worship me.*

10 *Then saith Jesus unto him, Get thee hence, Satan: for it is written, Thou shalt worship the Lord thy God, and him only shalt thou serve.*

11 *Then the devil leaveth him, and, behold, angels came and ministered unto him.*

This, my friend, is where the rubber met the road. It's what the devil really wanted more than anything and everything else. Forget turning stones to bread. Forget leaping off tall buildings to facilitate a game of catch among the angels. What the devil wanted in the worst way is for his nemesis, his arch enemy, his former friend and co-resident of heaven, Jesus, to—read these words carefully—"fall down and Worship me."

Furthermore, it's not so much that the devil wanted Jesus' Worship. It's much more sinister than that. The devil wasn't as interested in getting *at* Jesus as he was at getting *back* at Jesus' Father, God. This wasn't the first time Jesus and the devil had met. No, they had *history*. Jesus says in Luke 10:18, "I beheld Satan as lightning fall from heaven." In some respects, the devil was acting here like a jilted and petulant lover. God had ended their relationship abruptly, as recorded in Isaiah 14:12-14, KJV:

> 12 *How art thou fallen from heaven, O Lucifer, son of the morning! how art thou cut down to the ground, which didst weaken the nations!*
>
> 13 *For thou hast said in thine heart, I will ascend into heaven, I will exalt my throne above the stars of God: I will sit also upon the mount of the congregation, in the sides of the north:*
>
> 14 *I will ascend above the heights of the clouds; I will be like the most High.*

Talk about delusions of grandeur! The devil craves God's position. He wants to be like God. He hates God. And, like many a jilted lover, the devil's mantra is: "If I can't have you, nobody can have you." The devil didn't want Jesus' Worship; he just didn't want God to have it. And he doesn't want God to have your Worship either. But as I heard repeatedly said by many a seasoned saint during my childhood days, "The devil *is* a lie!" And Worship is a proven method of getting the devil to leave you, albeit temporarily. Matthew 4:11 describes what happens when we articulate and demonstrate an accurate understanding of Worship: *Then the devil leaveth him, and, behold, angels came and ministered unto him* (KJV). The devil exits and ministering angels enter!

There is another reason the devil doesn't want us to Worship God, and it has to do with what Worship does for the Worshiper. Worship isn't meant to be continuous. Worship is preparatory. Worship is a prelude (an action or event serving as an introduction to something more important[23]) to positive action on the part of the Worshiper. And this is where it becomes clear that the veil that appears to be covering the eyes of so many Christians regarding Worship is a matter of spiritual warfare. According to Ephesians 6:12, "we wrestle not against flesh and blood, but against principalities, against powers, against the rulers of the darkness of this world, against spiritual wickedness in high places" (KJV). The value of Worship can be clearly discerned by the level of confusion and ignorance surrounding it. Following is a verbatim reflection of an Instagram comments thread posted in response to a photograph released by NBC news under the caption, "Pope Francis lies down in prayer before the beginning of Good Friday service at the Vatican with the Passion of the Christ Mass at St. Peter's Basilica" (which may indicate that NBC news' copywriters are not really sure what Worship is!)[24]

Philadelphiamark: I'm Catholic, but am I the only one that finds this a little strange?

Gracy101: I'm also Catholic and I have never seen any pope do this. I have seen them kiss the floor when they arrive at new country, but never this. Also, went to Catholic school and I don't remember being taught this. Is he praying?

Spiritualawakening75: big strange.

Mojobubba: Roman Catholicism is NOT Christian!

Minellee2: yeah, religion is dangerous.

Shadowsmile27: This man's a clown.

Glitched_lie66: Someone call LIFE ALERT, because he has fallen and can't get up.

Acutebrat: Are we sure he didn't trip and play it off well so as not to seem fragile and weak?

Lasallewilliam: Pope Francis is only a politician and is neither a Christian nor a good person.

myssi1104: Laying on the magic carpet.

allrock3: He's the anti-Christ.

Wwjd_aw: What a show. And God doesn't honor any of it.

Eileen.stafford.54: I wouldn't be able to get up.

Tlackovitch: I always took a nap in church too!

Izatrinipheonix_75: He lays like the serpent that he is.

Chyco4j: Something is not right with this man.

Tonybacardi: When you pray, don't be like the hypocrites, for the love to pray in the churches and in the corners of the streets to be seen by men.—Matthew 6:5

Johnnyd_92: Wth??? Why? Jesus despised all these man made theatrics.

fabiom4870: Why do people follow this Man he covered for rapist why is that?

fern.taylorartist: At first I thought trump had succumbed to his fast food diet! So close.

katembo01: When you wanna pray to Allah but then you remember you're the Pope.

carloscarloscarlos_m: Laziest. Pope. Ever.

Danikirkman: Religion is so weird. All of them.

pedromartinez6837: 21st century, and still trying to deceive the sheep, what a moron, when are they gonna lock up all the cardinal pedophiles, or are still paying millions in hush money.

Katchatone: Wait…what is going on here?!?

cowboy_up72: He's a fraud and he will have to answer to God. He's not special or should by now down to him. Too bad millions of people are being deceived by him.

Mellowjaysmokin: Looks like he's waiting for the Priest to get on top of him.

lefty_zigzag: Lies down?

mando8352: CLOWN

str8evil: Any place is a good place for a power nap.

Biglynnie: Wonder how many men in this have molested children?

real_samuel_rm: "Y'all start the service without me, I need to rest my eyes".

suzanne4369: Foolish action.

miac2683: Why is he doing that?

~ ~ ~ ~ ~ ~ ~

I think you get the picture. Interestingly, many of the above comments are posted by people who identify themselves as Christians, some even as Catholics. One thing that is clear from most of the posts, aside from the sarcasm, vitriol, and seething contempt for the titular head of the Catholic Church, is the level of absolute collective ignorance as to the concept of Worship. I cannot overstress the significance of this. The Catholic Church is two millennia old![25] I said, the Catholic Church is TWO **THOUSAND** YEARS OLD! With all due respect, is it not reasonable to assume that someone, somewhere in all the catechisms, and confessions, and homilies, and papal bulls would instruct the adherents of the Catholic faith in how to Worship the God *of* the Catholic Church? Again, I take no pride in the fact that even Protestant denominations, including my own, have done such a poor job of teaching and modeling Worship. But as President Harry S. Truman once famously said, "The buck stops here!"[26] I am willing to take up the gauntlet to fight for the re-introduction of Worship into the Christian lexicon and practice, which it obviously was at one time. How is it possible that such an obvious component of the Christian faith could be hidden in plain sight for so long among so many who claim to follow Christ?

Let's revisit Twitter. On my weekly radio commentary during late Spring 2019, I opined over the airwaves that with Memphis having so many churches, aka "houses of Worship," I thought our city should be better and safer than it was at that time. At the end of the commentary, I asked my listeners to tweet their answers to the following question: "What is Worship?" Here are some of the responses:

@EasterwoodKeith: For me it's prayer and dialogue with god, I talk to him all day, hurts, pains, hopes, family etc.

@HendrenWade: I listened Brother! My one word is PRAYER!

@bdburks: An act of reverence and obedience to God.

@NebWeng: To recognize God's greatness!!!

@EvelynGreen1956: To give honor and respect to him that is worthy and forth right.

@__NikiLou__: Worship to me is a feeling or expression of love, adoration, reverence, esteem, exaltation, thankfulness, greatfulness, honor and respect to the most high God!

@bstkersa: There are different forms of worship. Worship of God is a religious belief that He is the Creator and you follow Him, you venerate Him and follow His teachings. To worship an individual is to think very highly of him and everything he does, you idolize him.

@JayCulpepper7: Wow. This is much more difficult to put into words than I imagined. Worship is rejoicing in God and telling how much you love and thank him. How thankful you are for him and all he has done for you. Personally, I think worship is not limited to a building and can be done anywhere.

@MrBigE88: Me showing the Lord (in my own way) how much He's 'WORTH' to me.

"Worship is the most under-developed, under-researched, and unappreciated biblical concept in all of Christendom."

CHAPTER SIX

$\sim$◦$\mathcal{O} \mathcal{S} \sim \mathcal{O}$◦$\sim$

"This is The Call
to Worship"

Every Sunday when congregants enter our sanctuary, they are handed a printed bulletin that includes our liturgical sequence. Inside the front cover is a page explaining what Worship is, for the benefit of those visitors in attendance who may not know, which usually is *all* of the visitors! Just before the opening prayer, which is led by one of our Deacons, a member of the church comes to the microphone and shares with those in attendance why he or she Worships God. They start by stating their name, then they explain in a few words why they engage in the practice of Worship. Then, they read the scripture of their choice. Next, they say, *"This is the call to Worship. You are instructed to come to the Altar and lay prostrate, bow, kneel, and/or blow kisses to God. Please note that this instruction is for everyone in our Sanctuary, including our visitors. God will bless you as you submit to the spiritual flow of this house. Again, this instruction is for everyone in this sanctuary, including our visitors. Remember to let the music drive your Worship. The end of the prayer is not the end of Worship. I repeat, the end of the prayer is not the end of Worship. When the Intercessor says 'amen' please do not stop Worshiping. Please continue to lay prostrate, bow, kneel, and/or blow kisses to God. When the music moves from Worship to praise, you move from Worship to praise. This is the call to Worship."*

On the inside front cover of the bulletin is the following detailed explanation:

Worship at The New Olivet Worship Center

- "You are instructed to come to the altar to lay prostrate, bow, kneel and/or blow kisses to God. This is the call to Worship."
- At The New Olivet, the call to Worship is a call to action. This action takes place at the Altar.
- The biblical definition of WORSHIP is to lay prostrate, bow, kneel, and/or blow kisses to God in homage (special honor shown publicly) and obeisance (a gesture expressing deferential respect)
- When you are in a position of Worship, you can listen with your heart and your ears to God speaking to you. You also can listen and agree with the prayers going forth from the pulpit.
- The Worship experience is enhanced through the burning of incense at the altar ("...and the smoke of the incense...came with the prayers of the saints"—Revelation 8:4).

The Altar itself is significant to Worship. The Altar is the place where we are "altar"ed. At the Altar you are free to Worship and praise Him. Come to the Altar every time the invitation is extended.

23 But the hour cometh, and now is, when the true worshipers shall worship the Father in spirit and in truth: for the Father seeketh such to worship him. 24 God is a Spirit: and they that worship him must worship him in spirit and in truth. John 4:23-24 KJV

On the same page are three photographs of me engaging in all three forms of Worship. I also physically lead the congregation in Worship. (It's very important that the Pastor lead by example in every aspect of congregational life, particularly with regard to liturgical matters. I know of many churches where the Pastor is not even in the sanctuary when the Worship service starts. Sometimes they don't even come in until just before it's time for them to preach. And they leave right after they preach, not taking time to interact with church attendees.)

On the following pages you will find several actual verbatim transcripts from members of our church. You will notice that they have not been "scrubbed" for errors. They have not been redacted or corrected. They have not been "spell-checked" or "grammar-checked." I have not even changed their "little w" references to "capital W." I just want you to feel the hearts of these beautiful people whose lives have been changed through their Worship in their own words! Each example begins with the name of the Worshiper in brackets.

{Debra} I must admit to you that in the beginning I did not worship God; at least not true worship, the kind that pleases God. When Pastor Whalum brought this to the congregation (even though worship is prevalent throughout the Bible; I was not with this program. I was a rebel without a cause, a stiff-necked people in my own right. Thinking that I already do enough; I sing, I clap, dance a little and occasionally open my mouth and give God verbal praise. Well, as long as I can remember worship and praise have always been pretty much joined at the hip and treated as one in the same. Then Pastor Whalum conducted "the workshop" revelation, and just think, it's been in the Word of God the whole time, the same word that I carry around in my car, have on my desk, on my nightstand, you get my drift. So now, I worship God out of obedience to Him, and I wanted to do something right for a change, prove my love to Him, please Him. I didn't want to continue feeling the pinch of conviction of disobedience to God and to the Prophet of this house when it was time for the call to worship or anytime for that matter. I worship Him because He is my Creator, my refuge, my Hope, my salvation, because He is Omnipotent (all powerful, supreme, invincible), Omniscient (all knowing) and Omnipresent (ubiquitous and universal). Because He kept me sane when I thought I was going to lose my mind (up in here) from all manner of circumstances. I keep holding on for dear life to His promises because I know my life, the lives of my children, and anybody I am connected to and come in contact with depends on it. I worship God because it is right and good!

{Valerie} My worship is the most personable act in my life. During the times when I thought my life was over due to lupus, my worship comforted me into a healthy state of being. We've all experienced a loss to death. I mean it's inevitable. But have you ever lost someone to life? I'm quite sure we have experienced that as well. Giving up my fourteen-year-old adopted daughter was and still is the hardest decision I've had to make in my life. During the tears, the indecisiveness, the stress, the abuse, and the feelings of hopelessness, my worship is the antiseptic that cleanses, soothes and heals my broken heart, soul, and body.

{Terry} Worship is an act of submission, and I want to show God that I surrender to His way and that I trust him with my life. Also, because he created and foresees my future, I acknowledge that he's always providing the way for me. I know that he loves me, and it's displayed every day. So, my worship is to show forth appreciation for what he's done, what he's doing, and for what is still yet to come. Worship is an opportunity to rest before God with any of my issues or concerns. To lay them before Him and know that all is well. Sometimes we are faced with challenges that may appear to be insurmountable, but through worship I gain strength in knowing that I'm more than capable through him that is in me.

I worship because God continues to guide me in loving my wife and conquering being a first-time parent. I worship to be equipped to carry out my duties as a Husband and as a Father. That I'm attentive and responsive to the needs of my wife and son. Because it's important that I create an atmosphere that is inspiring and uplifting. So, through worship I'm able to be supportive and provide for my family. Through worship God has shown me how to remain positive even when there are unfavorable outcomes. It allows me to have peace and not worry about the things that are beyond my control. I worship because God is faithful and when I lay prostrate, I ask GOD to sanctify my body so that my thoughts and emotions are aligned with His way. Worship allows me to remain confident that my relationship with God is secured and that I'm able to fulfill my commitment to him. Good Evening!

{Valerie #2} My topic is, "Not Blood Mothers." I am a 25-year Systemic Lupus survivor and a single adoptive mother of 3. Kristina is 19, Diamond is 15, and Kristian is 14. I also support my god-son Kierstan, who is 17, and my god-daughter Damali, who is 18. Kierstan and Damali were my foster children when they were 2 and 3 years old. So you don't foster and forget. Mother, motherhood, and mothering are defined in many ways in today's world. One definition states the word mother encompasses a woman's eternal role, her divine identity, and it describes her nature as a nurturer. With this perspective, women mother by not only giving physical life to a child, but also by nurturing those around them. To nurture is to provide love and influence, to care for, support, educate, encourage, to protect, and to teach. To nurture is to help someone grow and develop. Okay, we have all heard or even said ourselves that, "Blood is thicker than water." This often came about as children when we were in combat with other kids outside of the family and you were there to help your brother, sister, even cousin, to fight. But how many of us grown folk know that the saying isn't always so. I know from personal experience that I get more help from strangers, or since we are talking about blood, non-blood individuals than I can family. Understand that there is no love lost. Sometimes, you have to get in where you fit in. I am a frequent Facebooker, Instagrammer, and Tweeter, and I remember seeing and sharing a post that said, "No one supports you like that social media friend that you have never met." Know that your biggest supporter is not always going to be blood. As a non-blood mother, even when I'm battling my worst Lupus flares, I'm still supporting my children. I've had surgeries, sickness, and things not only uncontrollable but unimaginable happen to me, and I could not rely on blood to be there. Each one of my children have unique gifts and talents and I find myself sacrificing my own time, health, and finances to ensure a good quality of life for them. I always tell them that it is my job to make sure they all can have quality life in their adulthood. I have laid the foundation, now you build the house. To continue the conversation on, "Blood is thicker than water," did you know that it is okay to have a blood clot? In the medical field, we know that blood clots in most instances could lead to death. But in this case, if your blood family is not your nurturer and is more of a nuisance, then clot them off. There are so many children in the foster care and juvenile system in which the blood family has clot off. These children are emotional and mental wrecks. They are not seeing what God is doing in their little lives. All they want is family (Blood Family). I ask God right now to sanctify the separation. Let them realize the family that they are with may not be blood, but they are the life-line to their future. Then along comes the foster mothers and adoptive mothers, in essence, the non-blood mothers who try to transfuse or love away the pain, the insecurities, the feelings of abandonment. Sometimes we are successful, and sometimes we are not. Yeah, we too experience disrespect, physical abuse, verbal abuse, mental anguish, and defeat. But as non-blood mothers, we have to keep pressing and we have to keep praying. We must not give up. We are ALL adopted into the body of Christ. Jesus came so that we can have first abundant life and eternal life. When I think about adoption in the Bible, I think about Moses. Pharaoh's daughter took the Hebrew baby, who was sentenced to death and who was his non-blood mother and raised, loved, and nurtured him as her own. This is the first documentation of her blood (Pharaoh's daughter) is not thicker than the water of the Nile River, of which she found him in. But, because of the love, and care, and nurturing of his non-blood mother, Moses became a great man. Your most "beloved" is not always from your womb. I have 5, and they are all destined for greatness. Many often ask why I decided to foster and adopt. I love children. I feel that children are my calling and my purpose. Whitney said it best when she said, "I believe that children are the future, teach them well and let them lead the way...". Children are the Greatest Love of All. However, once diagnosed with Lupus in 1994, at the age of 24, I made the conscious decision not to have any biological children, but I always desired to be a mother. Don't get it twisted, motherhood is not an easy task, especially when they are not genetically yours. I'm a firm believer in discipline. After all, the saying goes, "Spare the rod, spoil the child." However, the Bible says in Proverbs 13:24, NIV, "Whoever spares the rod hates their children, but the one who loves their children is careful to discipline them." But sometimes, that form of discipline is not effective for all. In reality, you can't beat the DNA out of them. When children come from a gestational history of physical abuse, corporal punishment is not the best answer. When children come from a history of emotional and psychological abuse, corporal punishment is not the best answer. We non-blood mothers have to find an alternative method to correct the behaviors of that troubled child. Prayer, worship, therapy, counselors, mentorship, sports, creative arts such as dancing, modeling, acting, martial arts, and, of course, education. Sometimes, some children are unreachable no matter how hard you try. But when you know that you've done all you can, it is okay to release them or clot them off and give them back to God. Ask God to sanctify the separation, and in this circle of life, if it's in God's will, He will reunite the union and the relationship will be what God destined it to be. Just know that God can do exceedingly and abundantly all that we can ever ask or think. Now, what I am about to say absolutely has nothing to do with the topic of "Non-Blood Mothers," but it's relevant. I have had so many men and women come to me and say, "I couldn't do it. I don't want no one else's problem." Well my rebuttal is, "First of all, nobody is perfect." Then, I go on to say, "Be careful who you decide to have children with." Just because he is tall dark and handsome, or she looks like a model, or they have prefixes before or suffixes behind their names and they have nice homes and good jobs and appear to have it going on, did you check their DNA? Did you check the family tree? Now, three or four generations later, that behavior, that mental illness shows up in your blood-born child, and you are now going through the same struggles and backlash that we non-blood mothers are experiencing. I say to you, IT TAKES A VILLAGE! If the village don't raise them, the villains will. So how can the community help in supporting NON-BLOOD MOTHERS, SINGLE MOTHERS, 21ˢᵗ CENTURY MOTHERS, FORGOTTEN MOTHERS, CHURCH MOTHERS, TEEN MOTHERS or any other kind of mother? I'm glad you asked. You pray for us. You go down in worship for us. To Worship is to lay prostrate, bow, and/or kneel or blow kisses to God. 2 Chronicles 7:14, KJV says, "If my people which are called by my name, shall humble themselves and pray and seek my face and turn from their wicked ways, then will I hear from Heaven and will forgive their sins and heal their land." You can also help by being genuine. If you don't know our business, then mind your business. Don't get in our business and don't tear us down. Also listen with love and execute that returned love in a God-given fashion. Don't get caught up in gossip and the spirit of gossiping. Most important, give back. Give through food, clothing, time, and money, and love. I am the founder of a 501c3 NON-PROFIT called THE A.N.D.Y. PROJECT. ANDY stands for Assisting the NEEDS of Disadvantage Youths. My son, Kristian, is the co-founder and the inspiration behind the project. Andy was his birth name. Once adopted, at the age of three, I changed his name to Kristian. The ANDY

Project helps kids who are economically challenged in the community. This past school year we bless the pre-K classes at Hawkins Mill Elementary by reading weekly and providing gifts throughout the school year. And guess what, every mother that was talked about this month benefited from The Andy Project. In closing, I would like everyone to stand and repeat after me…"AM I MY MOTHER'S KEEPER?" Then say…"YES I AM!"

{Denise} My worship is for real. In the most challenging decade of my life, I had everything I wanted and lost everything that I had. But God, and the power of a worshipping Shepherd, sent a lamp unto my feet, an Angel who said, "I'll Go With You, Hold On," even when your strength is gone. My worship restored my belief in myself and allowed me to re-call who I am. A certain woman, rarely named, barely known but blessed with gifts and talents the world will make room to receive; An Abigail important to those who see her the same way God does, a gap stander. My worship has made me a better praiser, full of spirit. In the words of Smokie Norful, It may not be all that I'd hoped for, and every dream has not yet materialized, but my hope is built on nothing less, than HIS blood and righteousness. My facetime is an application, connecting me with the face of God and with my future self—the me where I am happy. Whole, prosperous, and living life abundantly. Worship is my hope-restorer, the source of my Daily Bread, the reason I can say blessings thou art showering, full and free, even me, Lord Worship will lead you to find Elle haddebarim, the words that will grow your faith.

{Celeste} I worship because when I chose to walk away and give up on Him, He never gave up on me. My life has had its challenges, and I did not believe I would ever be filled with the joy and happiness that I have today. I gave up on me, and in that, I gave up on God. I attempted suicide twice in my life because the pain that I felt was greater than the love for which I longed. I was striving in my own strength to make my life what I thought it was supposed to be and the pain was still there. I was blind to see that His hand and His love was upon me through the full walk. With all that I had done, how could such a great God love the flawed and broken pieces that had denied Him? How could I surrender and return to a God that was perfect in every way when all I could see were my own imperfections? But when I finally came to the end of myself and to the beginning of Him, He showed me that He always loved me, and He rocked me in the cradle of His arms. Now, even my worst days are great. He takes my brokenness, my flaws, and my imperfections and uses them for His glory. And out of that victory, He gave me my purpose. His unconditional love is why I worship.

{Jocelyn} I worship because God is helping me to become who I need to be. The more I worship, the more I recognize my ability to be and do. Because of my worship, I am anointed, and my cup runs over, and goodness and mercy are following me and shall follow me all the days of my life. Because of my worship, I have favor with God; He covers me, my family, my friends, and anyone I come in contact with. Because of my worship, I have a responsibility to cover and pray for the people that ask me to do so. The little 4-year-old boy that shot himself last week was the nephew of my friend from college. Now we don't talk as often as we should, but she sent me a message saying she felt she needed to let me know that this happened to her nephew and notified me of the arrangements, even though I had never met her nephew and hadn't really talked to her in a few years. But I know she wanted me to pray for her, and I replied with a prayer and prayed for her again right before the funeral on Saturday.

Because of my worship, I am strengthened and can be there for others. Because of my worship, I am blessed, committed, and faithful. I am learning to be faithful over what God has given me. Because of my worship, some years ago I took the financial freedom class. Since then, I have learned the hard lesson of only buying what I actually have the money to pay for and not being dependent on credit cards. Worship changes the way you think about yourself, about others, and about life. Lately, I have been asking God to enlarge my territory and increase my tithes and giving. And just this past week I was told by my boss to expect an increase in my salary. Now, this increase didn't come the way I thought it would, but it is still an increase and it comes with more responsibility. I know that because of my worship I will be able to handle both the increase and added responsibility.

Philippians 4:7; 13 says, "And the peace of God [that peace which reassures the heart, that peace] which transcends all understanding, [that peace which] stands guard over your hearts and your minds in Christ Jesus [is yours] I can do all things [which He has called me to do] through Him who strengthens and empowers me [to fulfill His purpose." I am self-sufficient in Christ's sufficiency; I am ready for anything and equal to anything through Him who infuses me with inner strength and confident peace.

{Marilyn} I worship because God has made me certain promises that deserves all my worship and all my praise. When I blow kisses, lay out prostate, or bow before the Lord I'm reminded HE told me He'd never leave me nor forsake me. I worship because HE told me that by Jesus' stripes I AM HEALED. I worship because He told me He knows the plans HE has for me; plans to prosper me and not to harm me. I worship because HE told me HE is my light and my salvation, whom shall I fear? I worship because HE told me If HE be for me than who shall be against me? I worship because HE told me that all things work together for good for those who love the LORD and who are called according to his purpose. I worship because HE told me HE is my SHEPHERD, and I shall not want. I worship because HE told me If I delight myself in HIM, HE will give me the desires of my heart. I worship because HE told me Greater is HE that is in me than HE that is in the world. I worship because HE told me that the effective, fervent prayer of a righteous man avails much. I worship because HE told me HIS word shall go forth from HIS mouth and it would not return to HIM void. I worship because HE told me If I wait upon HIM, I would get new strength and spread my wings and soar like an eagle. I worship because HE told me I can run and not get tired, walk and not lag behind. I worship because my life depends on it. I'm standing on HIS word trusting and believing. The scent of this woman is confidence, strength, and peace in the midst of the storm. I refuse to give up or give in to the lies or tricks of the enemy. I worship because I can speak to the storm and it has to cease. I worship because God maintains and keeps me. He loves me when I feel down and feel worried over things I have no control of. I've learned that God cares about some of the simplest things that I make into mountains. But with the grace He's given me, I worship and find where I need to tell that mountain to go.

{Stacie} I worship because it is honoring to God. He is my ALL in everything and besides striving to be that obedient child, true worship is the absolute most I can give Him. A couple of years ago…really into giving God what He craved at this point…some things began to happen, and I decided I wanted to go back to school. But with that, I had to leave my job because the program was really intense and hard. It was a real test of faith to trust God to keep me during those times, and I am grateful that He did. After graduating with honors, worshiping and praying the whole way through… I had a job immediately. It didn't last long, but it was what I needed when I needed it. I had applied to so many places and had several interviews…it was hard to keep track but still when nothing fell through when I wanted… I thought maybe it's just time for me to wait on whatever job God wanted me to have. So, while I waited, I enrolled into a bachelor's program at Bethel. Just a few weeks ago, I received a phone call from my old instructor. She said, "Stacie… I need a lab assistant and I thought about you. You have to go through the interview process, but I already told them who I wanted so don't worry about not meeting all of the requirements…" I gave thanks and worshipped, and then reflected on how it all came to pass. I met with my instructor and I had to ask her why there wasn't a lab assistant when my cohort was going through the program, and she looked at me and said… I just made it up.

{Melissa} I worship because I have a praying mother that instilled in me a love of Jesus at an early age. I worship because my biological father chose not to be in my life, and despite all of the negative emotions and ramifications that came along with that, it was through worship that I was able to forgive him and move on with my life and have peace and joy. I worship because God blessed me with a wonderful husband and a marriage that strengthens me and helps me to grow as a person. And it's because of worship that we just celebrated 18 years this past December. I worship because I have been tasked with the important role of being the mother of 3 black boys, future black men in today's society. Knowing everything that awaits them in the world, it's because of worship that I have peace in knowing that angels encamp all around them, keeping them safe from all hurt, harm, and danger! I worship because I have the daughter of my dreams. I worship because God put a dream in my heart to sing and dance from a young age, and it's because of worship that I have been able to make a living as a performer for the past 20 years. I worship because my youngest son has sickle cell and even though it can be very serious, he is healthy and thriving thanks in part to the care he receives at St. Jude. The medicine they prescribed has made his blood levels normal, and he only had two hospital stays in 2017. This is why I worship.

{Nicole} I Worship because when it was introduced to me back in 2009, I didn't receive it. God had instructed where to go and gave me the tools to move to the next level, but I ignored the teachings. You know, we all have storms and storms come to interrupt things. It will move things out of your life, make you think differently, and get you focused on the main thing. I continued to call out to God for help, and He told me to Worship. You see, I was in the house but ignoring the teachings. When I got in tune with the Holy Spirit the frequency got clearer. When I surrendered to God and went to the altar, my life has never been the same. When I laid prostrate at the altar my heart was relieved; my soul was happy; my mind was clearer, and my lifestyle was brand new. Worship consecrates my mind and helped me to understand the guidance that's within me to get me to the next level. I Worship because as the storms continue to come, and they will, worship helps me to feel how I feel but move when God says move. Worship works. I promise you, Worship works, and this is the reason why I Worship.

{Tammie} I Worship because I want to give God what He wants, and He craves Worship. I worship God because He is LORD of my life, capital L, capital O, capital R, capital D. I worship God because I want to honor Him in the purest way, by humbling myself and surrendering all that is me: my body, thoughts, and spirit to My LORD. I worship God because He is amazingly awesome! I also worship because I get to reap the benefits of it. Earlier this year, I became unemployed when the government shutdown. But God gave me another job in my field with increase that I love, and I receive favor from them daily. God has restored family relationships and is restoring relationships. And although I am facing some medical concerns, my God through worship has given me a peace that everything will be fine. Worship gives me a sense of certainty that all is well; this is why I worship.

"Worship is the most under-developed, under-researched, and unappreciated biblical concept in all of Christendom."

CHAPTER SEVEN

Letter From Birmingham Jail {Except I'm Not In Birmingham, And I'm Not In A Literal Jail Cell!}

No, I'm not in Birmingham, and I'm not in a literal jail cell as Dr. Martin Luther King, Jr. was when he wrote his famously searing "Letter from Birmingham Jail." But I *am* in the same mood of righteous indignation and impatience. Dr. King wrote the letter in 1963 in response to published criticisms styled as a "public statement of concern" from a group of eight maddeningly conservative White religious leaders in the South.[27] Their collective counsel to Dr. King was that he should go slow in his attempts to overthrow the South's system of Jim Crow segregation through his non-violent direct-action tactics. Most White clergy and a growing number of Black clergy were put off by King's insistence on leading demonstrations which invariably led to the mass arrests and jailing of hundreds of Black Christians, sometimes even of children. His response was a brilliant and anointed articulation of why time was out for waiting. I feel same way when it comes to pastors and preachers who are either ignorant of the true meaning of Worship or unwilling to practice and teach it despite clear biblical evidence that God craves it.

Dr. Martin Luther King, Jr. was, first and foremost, a preacher of the gospel of Jesus Christ. Before he was a world leader. Before he won the Nobel Peace Prize. Before he even got his doctorate degree, he was a "Reverend." He was a preacher who was anointed for the task that God had placed before him. A few weeks before he preached his prescient "Mountaintop" sermon at Mason Temple Church of God in Christ in Memphis on April 3, 1968, he preached a sermon entitled, "God Is Able." Reader, do you believe God is able? He said these words during that sermon: "The God whom we Worship is not a weak and incompetent God. He is able to beat back gigantic waves of opposition, and to bring low prodigious mountains of evil. The ringing testimony of the Christian faith is that God is able." And Dr. King understood that the trigger to God's ability was the Worship of God's people. Yet, the next day, on April 4th, a demonic assassin took his life. Martin's blood still cries out from that balcony at the Lorraine Motel, which has been reborn as the National Civil Rights Museum at The Lorraine Motel. And I believe his blood is asking the question, "What is Memphis going to do with the knowledge that our Worship is not wasted?"

During the "Mountaintop" sermon he also said the following: "You know what's beautiful to me? It's to see all these ministers of the gospel here tonight. It's a marvelous thing!" It's a marvelous thing when preachers of the gospel get together on one accord. King knew that fateful night that he was addressing the ones responsible for teaching our people how to Worship, so that the full power of God could be released in the earth. Because "the God we Worship is not a weak and incompetent God." He was primarily talking to preachers that night. If he was right when he said the God we Worship is not a weak and incompetent God, and if that same God is able to bring low prodigious mountains of evil, if He can do all that, then the key must be our Worship. So, if there are still mountains of evil around us; if people are still killing their own babies (through abortion and otherwise); and if people are still killing people they know, and if nations are still rising up against nation, then there is still some evil that needs to come down! God is still able. There must be some things God's *people* are not doing. Dr. King suggested that Worship will make it happen. Let's go deeper.

Early in the "Mountaintop" sermon Dr. King said, "If God gave me the opportunity, I would take a mental flight down by Mount Olympus." That's in Greece. He continued, "I would see Plato, Aristotle, Socrates, Euripides, and Aristophanes gathered around the Parthenon." Why would Dr. King, in a meeting of Black preachers in Memphis, Tennessee, talk about Greece? I'll tell you why. It's because the Greek language is the original translation of the Hebrew text, which is the original translation of the Bible. The word of God must be understood in Greek to convey God's original intent, thus my detailed treatment of the Greek meaning of Worship. The ironic thing about it is that by the time of his assassination, the day after the "Mountaintop" sermon, a growing number of Black preachers increasingly criticized and ostracized King. By that time, he was lonely, disenchanted, and disgusted with what his dream had become. Many of the friends who surrounded him during his famous "I Have a Dream" speech on the steps of the Lincoln Memorial, in

August of 1963, had long deserted him by the time he got to Memphis. He was frustrated. So much so that in a televised interview he told an NBC reporter, Sander Vanocur, "I must confess that the dream that I had that day has in many points turned into a nightmare."[28] It was the same sense of dejection he had felt sitting behind the bars of that Birmingham jail cell, except now it wasn't generated by White clergy, but those of his own race and religion. (I elaborated on Dr. King's understanding of Worship in 2018 when I was keynote speaker at an annual Martin Luther King, Jr. Day event held at Brown Baptist Church, a Southern Baptist congregation in Olive Branch, Mississippi. The link to the video presentation is included in the endnotes.)[29]

As a self-proclaimed apostle of Worship, I am familiar with that frustration with the seemingly deaf ears of my co-laborers in the field of ministry, thus my letter:

Dear Pastors & Preachers:

Over the past several years, I have conducted a series of true Worship conferences for Pastors and preachers. The word "true" indicates that there is some other kind of Worship. If it is possible to have "true" Worship, then it is also possible to have "false" Worship. Please be mindful that it is possible to Worship God in something other than truth, something other than what God requires, something other than what God approves. It is possible to have false Worship. And I want you to understand that God will allow us to engage in false Worship. He's not going to reverse our habits. He's not going to stop us from doing what we're doing, even if it's wrong, even if it's not according to His will. That's why He gave us free will. He will allow us to do what it is we want to do. That's what it means to be free. Please keep that in mind as you contemplate what it means to Worship God and what your role is, has been, and will be in conveying that meaning to God's people. I chose the means of conferences because of what a conference is, in fact. The word conference means, "a formal meeting or discussion." It is time we convened formal meetings and formal discussions around the meaning of Worship and its place in the life of the churches we Pastor. Time is out for playing church. I said it's time to stop playing church. It's time for the Church to tell the world how to operate. Time is out for the Church asking the world for permission to be the Church. It's no longer time for the world to tell the Church what to do. It's time for the Church to tell the world what to do. I am aware that some of you may feel a little squeamish about this concept, so take a moment and repeat aloud those words: "It's time for the Church to tell the world what to do!" This is serious business. Why on earth would we have all this Dunamis power, all this spiritual dynamite power, and still be walking around on our tiptoes, afraid to engage and confront the world's systems? It's time to take charge. I said, it's time to take charge, Pastors! It's time to stop walking around nervous about your prophetic place in society. Be prophetic, not pathetic. It's time to stand up, be men and women of God, and take charge by changing the trajectory of our world. God gave us dominion over the earth. That means we are in charge. The reason I'm addressing Pastors and preachers is because it is best that we usher Worship in from the top, meaning from the earthly headship of the church, the pulpit, the Pastors given by God to the churches. But if it must be ushered in from the bottom, meaning the pews and lay membership, then so be it. If the Pastors and preachers aren't ready to do it like God said, then "we the people" are going to have to do it like God said.

Sincerely,
Your Brother and Son in Ministry:
Dr. Kenneth Twigg Whalum, Jr.

This book is serious business, and writing it is a significant step to take for a Black Baptist preacher who grew up in the Black Baptist Church in the deep South, complete with her staunch religious traditions. Those religious traditions include printed programs—called bulletins—wherein the phrase "Call to Worship" figures prominently, and where the altar is the most sacred space in every church building. By the way, that geographical distinction—"in the deep South"—is necessary to convey the gravitas of one of this book's major premises, which is that very few churches, including Black churches, actually practice true Worship. The Black Church in the United States is literally a descendant or offshoot of the White Church in the United States. If the White Church had practiced biblical Worship before, during, or after slavery, then perhaps the atrocities thereof would have been minimized. Perhaps they might never have occurred. But, alas, I'm getting ahead of myself. Bear with me, please. No discussion of Worship, or religion, or politics, or economics, or education, present, past, or future in the United States would be complete without considering the peculiar history of Black people in America. Worship, or the lack thereof, has been, and will continue to be, a foundational component to our nation's destiny. And that's why most church folk don't get it. The devil doesn't mind us shouting, crying, praising, dancing, preaching, praying, and singing. That doesn't bother him in the least bit. He just doesn't want us Worshiping our Father God.

"Worship is the most under-developed, under-researched, and unappreciated biblical concept in all of Christendom."

The information you're receiving from this book obligates you to act, one way or another. Before you continue reading, please do me a favor. Please check your own Bible for John 4:23. I'm not being facetious. Bear with me. When you get it, read it aloud. I'll wait…! Okay, you done? The only thing, according to your Bible and mine, that God is craving like a junkie is Worship. There is not one other activity on our part that God is craving. My dad was Pastor of several churches. In all the churches I attended growing up in Black Baptist and African Methodist Episcopal churches, I heard Worship talked about a lot. But I never, never, ever saw Worship practiced. And I never heard it taught. You may have (somehow, I doubt it!) but I didn't. Do you understand how important that statement is, coming from a Baptist Pastor? I referred earlier to Martin Luther King, Jr.'s April 3, 1968 "Mountaintop" sermon. During that same message, he uttered the following diagnosis of the spiritual health of America's body politic: "The nation is sick. Trouble is in the land; confusion all around."[30] The word "sick" means (1) affected by physical or mental illness; (2)disappointed, mortified, or miserable; (3)intensely annoyed with or bored by someone or something as a result of having had too much of them; (4)having abnormal or unnatural tendencies; (5)perverted; (6)*of an organization, system, or society suffering from serious problems, especially of a financial nature.*[31] Using the foregoing definitional nuances I'd like to agree with Dr. King and suggest that not only was our nation sick in 1968; our nation is *still* sick.

America's sickness is physical, mental, and spiritual. It is also financial, but in a way that is connected somehow to the other three. And every bit of America's sickness is rooted in race. What qualified Martin King to make the diagnosis in the first place was his unquestioned position as prophetic overseer of the prolific and prodigious period known as the Civil Rights Movement. Make no mistake about it, other than the Reconstruction Era, which lasted from roughly 1863 to 1877 as the United States government's official codified attempt to remedy and redress the systemic inequities of slavery and its political, social, and economic legacy, the Civil Rights Movement was the most successful struggle to attain and enforce constitutional, legal, civil, and human rights in the history of the world. The inarguable fact of the matter, as documented in the annals of American history through print media, audio tape, film, and otherwise, is that the leadership of the said movement emanated from the Black Church. Dr. King was the leader of the leaders, and his predominant inner motivation was his understanding of Worship. He once wrote, "Worship at its best is a social experience with people of all levels of life coming together to realize their oneness and unity under God."[32] His existential philosophy of Worship made it easy for Dr. King to connect with Gandhi's philosophy of nonviolence, even though King and Gandhi were of different religious affiliations. Part of the reason why Dr. King was able to motivate children, in all their innocence, to become "freedom fighters" and embrace Christian principles was, undoubtedly, his belief that "Worship is as natural to the human family as the rising of the sun to the cosmic order."[33]

America's sickness within the Black community can be likened to some form of PTSD (post-traumatic stress disorder), which sometimes manifests in the form of denial.[34] I'll say more about how this sickness affects the White community in a subsequent chapter, but for now let's examine a bit more closely how our common past still affects our present and prospects for our future. If it is true that Worship is as natural to the human family as the rising of the sun to the cosmic order—and I believe it is—then there appears to have been an eclipse of the sun, because there is so little Worship being practiced in the churches where it should be most prevalent. I referred earlier to our churches printing bulletins that contain numerous references to Worship. During my research for this book, I traveled to Birmingham and Montgomery, Alabama to visit the sites that were so important to the Civil Rights Movement. While in Birmingham, I attended Sunday services at Sixteenth Street Baptist Church where, on September 15, 1963, a terrorist bombing took the lives of four little girls who were preparing for Sunday School class. Somehow, I felt that surely Dr. King's understanding of the transformative power of Worship would permeate the atmosphere in such sacred spaces. I enjoyed the service, including the music and preaching, and the members of the church were warm and welcoming. The printed bulletin did, of course, have several references to Worship. On the

inside front cover, the first bullet point in a printed paragraph titled PHILOSOPHY OF MINISTRY read, "Exalt
the Savior through dynamic worship." I wondered what the
term "dynamic worship" meant. I hoped it meant that true
Worship was part of Sixteenth Street's ecclesiastical culture. I
would soon find out. The next page of the bulletin listed the
liturgical sequence, and the first two lines looked like this:

DYNAMIC WORSHIP

PRAISE AND

WORSHIP...................................*Praise Team*

Well, consider my bubble burst! It was clear that there
was no official clarity regarding the difference between praise
and Worship. During the pastoral comments before the
offertory the Pastor said, "And now we want to *worship* God
with our giving." Again, more proof that the following statement is true:

*"Worship is the most under-developed, under-researched,
and unappreciated biblical concept in all of Christendom."*

Toward the end of the Pastor's sermon, I wrote the following two questions in the margin of the bulletin page: "To
whom does Worship matter?" and "To whom *should* it matter?" I do not know the answer to the first question other than
to say it matters to me. Seemingly it doesn't matter to a lot
of churchgoers, though. The answer to the second question
is that it *should* matter to every person who is a Christian. It
should matter because Jesus taught that God the Father is
seeking true Worshipers. It should matter because Worship
is not an end in itself. Worship is a means *to* an end. "What
end?", you may ask. Let's go deeper.

CHAPTER EIGHT

—◦◦◦◦—

Again, I Say, Our Nation is "Sick"

I wrote in the previous chapter that I agree with Dr. Martin Luther King, Jr.'s assessment that the United States is sick, and that often this sickness manifests itself in the form of denial among Black people. This malady is even more evident among White Americans. The clinical definition of denial is, "a psychological defense mechanism in which confrontation with a personal problem or with reality is avoided by denying the existence of the problem or reality."[35] Denial is further defined as:

> a defense mechanism in which unpleasant thoughts, feelings, wishes, or events are ignored or excluded from conscious awareness. It may take such forms as refusal to acknowledge the reality of a terminal illness, a financial problem, an addiction, or a partner's infidelity. Denial

is an unconscious process that functions
to resolve emotional conflict or reduce
anxiety.[36]

Most White Americans apparently get very defensive
whenever the issue of race is brought up within the context
of *White Supremacy*, which is "the belief that the White race
is inherently superior to other races and that White people
should have control over people of other races."[37] Most often,
this defensive reaction surfaces during discussions of reparations, which is a form of redress to the descendants of slavery. The common response from White Americans is that
because slavery ended two hundred years ago, and because
no living White American owned slaves, nothing is owed to
the descendants of slaves. They think that the passage of time
is enough to erase the generational ravages triggered by that
horrific institution. That, my friend, is a form of denial. But
I agree with David Brooks, Op-Ed columnist for the New
York Times, who when writing about the racial divide in the
American experience said that it is "born out of sin".[38] He
opines further, "We don't talk about sin much in the public square anymore. But I don't think one can grasp the full
amplitude of racial injustice without invoking the darkest
impulses of human nature."[39] Those dark impulses mentioned by Mr. Brooks seem to be having their way in 21st
century America. Mass shootings/murders on American soil
by Americans—Black and White—are increasingly becom-
ing a horrible norm. I cannot recount them all but consider
this: Within a twenty-four-hour period as I was writing this
book there were two mass shootings resulting in thirty-one
deaths; one in El Paso, Texas, and the other in Dayton, Ohio.
In El Paso, where twenty two people were killed, police said
they found an anti-immigrant document espousing White

nationalist and racist views, which they believe was written by the suspect.[40] Again, I cannot recount all the instances similar to this one, but just know that White racism has been a major causative factor in dozens of such incidents.

Yes, our nation's sickness can be summed up in a word: Sin. And with that being the case, the only cure is to seek God's face through Worship.

"Worship is the most under-developed, under-researched, and unappreciated biblical concept in all of Christendom."

CHAPTER NINE

⊸◦⟨∽⟩◦⊶

The Blind Leading the Blind

Sometimes it seems that there is a veil covering the eyes of the Church when it comes to the issue of Worship. If Worship is the most under-developed, under-researched, and unappreciated biblical concept in all of Christendom, it is because Christendom actively resists its development, research, and appreciation. Speaking of Christendom, which is defined generally as "the worldwide body or society of Christians",[41] in its historical sense, the term usually refers to the Middle Ages and to the Early Modern period during which the Christian world represented a geopolitical power that was juxtaposed with both the pagan and especially the Muslim world.[42] There is a difference between Christendom and Christianity. The difference is subtle, but it is an important difference with an equally important distinction. Christianity is defined as the religion based on the person and teachings of Jesus of Nazareth or its beliefs and practices.[43] It is easy to envision instances where the body or "society" of Christians may have developed beliefs, doctrines, and practices that don't fully align with the beliefs, doctrines, and practices established for

Christianity by Christ himself. The relevant text is referenced elsewhere in this book, but it deserves a closer look. It's found in Mark 7:6-9 [KJV].

> 6 *He answered and said unto them, Well hath Esaias prophesied of you hypocrites, as it is written, This people honoureth me with their lips, but their heart is far from me.*
>
> 7 *Howbeit in vain do they worship me, teaching for doctrines the commandments of men.*
>
> 8 *For laying aside the commandment of God, ye hold the tradition of men, as the washing of pots and cups: and many other such like things ye do.*
>
> 9 And he said unto them, *Full well ye reject the commandment of God, that ye may keep you own tradition.*

Interestingly, Jesus characterizes hypocrisy in the context of Worship. Hypocrisy is a form of intentional spiritual blindness in which the hypocrite *chooses* not to see certain things. In a real sense, then, church leaders who don't understand what true Worship is are blind leaders. And there are no leaders without followers. Thus, in respect to Worship, the only thing God craves like a junkie, the blind are leading the blind. This applies to the thought leaders of Christendom, the revered scholars and theologians who have contributed to the vast trove of academic texts.

Why is there so little scholarly research on Worship as clearly delineated by Jesus? The only explanation is a voluntary and well-meaning ignorance of scripture. This well-meaning ignorance manifests itself in the collective thought life and practical ministry (aka *tradition*) of the Church, and it is inculcated into the curriculum of seminaries and Bible colleges, which are the training ground for future church Pastors, teachers, and laity. I include now an excerpt from the *Dictionary of Pastoral Care and Counseling* to illustrate my point:

> WORSHIP AND CELEBRATION. Worship, broadly defined, is the human response of praise, adoration, thanksgiving, and supplication to the mystery of God's being and self-communication. The activity of worship characteristically takes place within a gathered community of faith, involving time, space, symbols, ritual actions, speaking, music, and silence. Authentic worship both forms and expresses human beings in relation to the Divine.[44]

The degree to which the foregoing definition is missing the actual point when it comes to what Worship is, is self-evident. There are other instances of scholarly misdirection when it comes to the topic of Worship. Consider the following definition of Worship included in a textbook commonly assigned as curriculum material at seminaries.

> WORSHIP (From Old English *weorth-scipe*, "worth-ship" The service of praise, adoration, thanksgiving, and petition directed toward God through actions and attitudes. Christian worship is Trinitarian in form as praise is offered to God through Jesus Christ by the power of the Holy Spirit. PUBLIC WORSHIP

is the open worship and praise of God by
an assembly of Christian believers.[45]

Be honest; if you were confused about the definition of
Worship before you read the preceding definition, wouldn't
you be even more confused after reading it? My initial reaction after reading it the first time was, "Huh?!?!?"

*"Worship is the most under-developed, under-researched,
and unappreciated biblical concept in all of Christendom."*

CHAPTER TEN

Worship Is A Three-Legged Stool

Worship theory is a theological construct. Theory is defined as, "a supposition or a system of ideas intended to explain something, especially one based on general principles independent of the thing to be explained."[46] Theology, in short, simply means "thinking about God." The book you're reading is a detailed exploration of my thinking about God in the context of the one thing God craves from us: Worship. A construct is "an idea or theory containing various conceptual elements, typically one considered to be subjective and not based on empirical evidence."[47] The concept of Worship must be understood by faith, which by definition is antithetical to the notion of empirical evidence. As famously articulated in scripture, "faith is the substance of things hoped for, the evidence of things not seen."[48]

True Worship is a three-legged stool. There is a biblical basis for our understanding of Worship as it relates to the trajectory of the body of Christ today. The altar plays a crucial role in all this. "What altar?", you may ask. The altar in each local church (and the one you may have created in your home). Recent church attendance statistics, notwithstanding church membership and church mobilization, will be very important to the spiritual awakening and healing of our nation. According to a recent Gallop poll, the percentage of United States adults who belong to a church or other religious institution plummeted twenty percentage points between 1999 and 2018, hitting a low of fifty percent in 2018, which was down from a robust seventy percent in 1999. And as of 2019, the percentage had dipped *below* fifty percent![49] Interestingly, a growing number of Americans included in the percentage of people who don't go to church, consider themselves "spiritual, but not religious."[50] But if we are to heal and transform our nation, we're going to need to do it from a position of unity in corporate Worship. Hebrews 10:24,25 sets forth the reason we should gather on a regular basis in churches/houses of Worship:

24 *And let us consider one another to provoke unto love and to good works:*
25 *Not forsaking the assembling of ourselves together, as the manner of some is; but exhorting one another; and so much the more, as ye see the day approaching.*

The importance of church attendance, then, at least when it comes to the efficacy of Worship, cannot be overstated. Regardless of the prevailing social mores and free-wheeling theories about why people don't go to church, those of us who <u>*do*</u> go must be laser-focused on our attention to Worship when we gather in our sanctuaries, because the stakes are higher than they've ever been. There are three Bible passages that form the ideological structure of the three-legged stool of Worship.

Without all three of those legs, the stool in the diagram above would be useless. It would teeter, totter, and eventually tumble. No one could sit on it, let alone stand on it to reach a higher level. All three legs are needed to provide the balance of the stool. All three of the following passages, taken together, inform the notion that Worship is not an end unto itself, but a means to an end. I'll state the passages first, then unpack them. They are John 4:23 (as we have discussed previously), Matthew 23:19,20, and 2 Chronicles 7:14.

Leg #1—John 4:23, *But the hour cometh, and now is, when the true worshippers shall worship the Father in spirit and in truth: for the Father seeketh such to worship him.*

Leg #2—Matthew 23:19-20, *Ye fools and blind: for whether is greater, the gift, or the altar that sanctifieth the gift? Whoso therefore shall swear by the altar, sweareth by it, and by all things thereon.*

Leg #3—2 Chronicles 7:14, *If my people, which are called by my name, shall humble themselves, and pray, and seek my face, and turn from their wicked ways, then will I hear from heaven, and will forgive their sin, and will heal their land.*

Again, we've already discussed at length what Worship is, the importance of Worship, and why we should give our Worship to God. Leg #2 is no less important, not because of the effect it has on God, but because of the effect it has on the Worshiper. Jesus suggests in Matthew 23:19,20 that the altar has a sanctifying effect on everything that is placed on it. He was addressing a crowd of people that included Pharisees, his archenemies. The previous three verses provide the context for his teaching on the effects of the altar. Let's read them:

> 16 *"Woe to you, blind guides! You say, 'If anyone swears by the temple, it means nothing; but anyone who swears by the gold of the temple is bound by that oath.'*
>
> 17 *You blind fools! Which is greater: the gold, or the temple that makes the gold sacred?*
>
> 18 *You also say, 'If anyone swears by the altar, it means nothing; but anyone who swears by the gift on the altar is bound by that oath.'*

It is obvious from these verses that the temple altar was a sacred space for the Jews. Jesus' biting sarcasm in calling the Pharisees, well-respected religious leaders of their day, "blind guides" and "blind fools" highlights their hypocrisy in dealing with so important a space as the altar. In verse 19, and again in verse 20, Jesus ascribes to the altar a power heretofore reserved for God the Father and God the Holy Spirit; that is the power to sanctify: "Ye fools and blind: for whether is greater, the gift, or the altar that *sanctifieth* the gift?" The word sanctify, in Greek, is multifaceted. It means to acknowledge, to purify (or process), and to render.[51] I've assigned an acronym which I think is appropriate because of the compound benefits of Worship. The acronym is APR, which is actually a financial term which means "annual percentage rate," the rate at which interest is determined. Interest is another word for increase. The result of our Worship is that God increases us. Let's analyze the three components.

ACKNOWLEDGE= to accept or admit the existence or truth of. When we Worship God, he does not condemn us for our truth. He accepts and admits the existence of our truth, whatever that truth happens to be.[52]

PURIFY (or PROCESS)= to extract contaminants from, thereby making fit for consumption. The process of purification is not a pain-free one.[53]

RENDER= to deliver; to provide or give; to cause to be or become.[54]

"Worship is the most under-developed, under-researched, and unappreciated biblical concept in all of Christendom."

CHAPTER ELEVEN

Worship is Not An End; It's A Means To An End

Worship is not an end in itself; it's a means to an end. The mindset that has taken hold among most Christians, knowingly or not, is that church attendance fulfills our responsibility to God, and that our weekly aim should be to make it through said week until we can get to church. I have heard it said that church should be a hospital where the sick can be healed, and it is that. I have also heard it said that church should be like a gas station (what we used to refer to as "filling stations") where we go to get filled with the Spirit, or hope, or knowledge. But those analogies are incomplete. People who are healed at the hospital don't just stay in the hospital taking up bed space. They don't just go home and wait until they get sick again. They go about their lives, trying to live productively. People who fill up at the gas station don't just sit there idling at the pump until all the gas runs out and they need gas again. They drive off to their many destinations. Something should happen in our lives as a result of church attendance. Our trajectory should be affected in a positive way. The same is true of Worship. Certain things happen as a result of our Worship, and we should expect them to. It would be nonsensical to believe that God would be unaffected by receiving the one thing that He craves. We should expect God to react favorably to those who give Him what He craves. There are several examples of this in scripture. Take John 12:20-26 (KJV), for instance:

20 *And there were certain Greeks among them that came up to worship at the feast:*

21 *The same came therefore to Philip, which was of Bethsaida of Galilee, and desired him, saying, Sir, we would see Jesus.*

22 *Philip cometh and telleth Andrew: and again, Andrew and Philip tell Jesus.*

23 *And Jesus answered them, saying, The hour is come, that the Son of man should be glorified.*

24 *Verily, verily, I say unto you, Except a corn of wheat fall into the ground and die, it abideth alone: but if it die, it bringeth forth much fruit.*

25 *He that loveth his life shall lose it; and he that hateth his life in this world shall keep it unto life eternal.*

26 *If any man serve me, let him follow me; and where I am, there shall also my servant be: if any man serve me, him will my Father honour.*

Worship's greatest value is that it consecrates the mind. There is something to be said for the clarity achieved through the mindful meditation that is Worship. Worship elevates our thinking. And when our thinking is elevated so should be our expectations. After your mindset has been elevated there are certain benefits you should expect. Once you've come up to a higher elevation you can see the horizon more clearly. Your perspective changes when the quality of your thought life improves. In many ways, we are what we think about. The text says, "there were certain Greeks among them that came *up* to worship at the feast." Whenever you come up to an appreciation and understanding of Worship, certain things are about to happen in your life. Your priorities will begin to be ordered around your Worship. It is not a linguistic coincidence that these Greeks, who were not Jews, are described as coming *up* to Worship. And after they came up, their desire to see Jesus was fulfilled. The same will happen in your life! But they didn't just see Jesus, He communed with them and communicated certain truths to them. These were truths that the Jews had rejected up to this point. There is always revelation attached to Worship. Jesus *revealed* to them that the hour of His crucifixion was at hand. He *related* the principle of seedtime and harvest to His resurrection. And He *reassured* them that by sacrificially following Him, they would be honored by God. All because of their decision to go up to Worship! Worship, for them, was not an end in itself; it was a means to an end.

As I said, Worship's greatest value is that it consecrates the mind. Worship consecrates our minds to *appreciate* our sonship (and daughtership) in God. Worship consecrates our minds to *allow* Jesus to fulfil God's plan for our lives. Worship consecrates our minds to *adjust* our prayers to fit our personalities. Worship consecrates our minds to *acknowledge* other folks' blessings without questioning the source of the blessings. Worship consecrates our minds to *accept* the mantle of spiritual warfare. Worship consecrates our minds to *agree* with God's authority. Worship consecrates our minds to *anticipate* Christ's return.

"Worship is the most under-developed, under-researched, and unappreciated biblical concept in all of Christendom."

CHAPTER TWELVE

Worship is Warfare

It is impossible to win a war if you don't know who your enemies are. I'd like to say a few things about this notion that Worship is warfare. My church's mission is to be "the preeminent church for the teaching of true Worship." Do you remember the television series, and more recently the movie series, entitled *Mission Impossible*? In the opening scene of the show there would be a voice that would say to the protagonist spy Ethan Hunt, "Your mission, should you decide to accept it, is…". Then the cassette tape on which the instructions were contained would self-destruct, going up in a cloud of smoke. I have decided to accept the mission of being Pastor of the preeminent church for the teaching of true Worship. That's a spiritually militant mission, and the degree to which our church, or your church, is successful in carrying out the mission depends entirely upon our willingness to accept the mission. It's a unique mission as well when one considers what most churches stand for or spend most of their time pursuing. It has been my experience that most churches, specifically Black churches, deal more with getting people ready for Heaven than getting people ready to make Heaven real on earth. It seems to me that our churches—Black and White—tend to be focused more on *having* church than *being* church, and most Christians are very uncomfortable being confronted with clearly biblical indications that we are engaged in spiritual warfare.

Add to that the incontrovertible fact, also biblical, that churchgoing people often allow our religious traditions to have authority over and above what the Bible clearly says, and you have a recipe for confusion, denial, and delay in changing our behavior and trajectory. This can also be a recipe for tension in our relationship with family, friends, co-workers, and others. Think about it: how do you tell a person who thinks they are Worshiping that they are not Worshiping according to what the Christ of the Bible says about Worship? Any time you take that kind of stand you're going to be opposed, and rejected, and ostracized, and talked about, and marginalized, and laughed at. People will say all manner of evil against you falsely because you have the temerity to believe and articulate something that goes against the grain of tradition. My advice to you is: R-E-L-A-X. Jesus promised that we would experience this tension in following him. Listen to what he says in Matthew 10:34-37.

34 *Think not that I am come to send peace on earth: I came not to send peace, but a sword.*

35 *For I am come to set a man at variance against his father, and the daughter against her mother, and the daughter in law against her mother in law.*

36 *And a man's foes shall be they of his own household.*

37 *He that loveth father or mother more than me is not worthy of me: and he that loveth son or daughter more than me is not worthy of me.*

Yes, spiritual warfare exists even among families. Warfare is serious business, and we can't choose our battles. Spiritual warfare is not a game. The devil is real, and the stakes are high.

"Worship is the most under-developed, under-researched, and unappreciated biblical concept in all of Christendom."

CHAPTER THIRTEEN

---∞◦◦◦◦∞---

Arrows Up!

Psalm 127:4 says, "As arrows are in the hand of a mighty man; so are children of the youth." We have adopted this biblical metaphor as appropriate to how Christians ought to rear their children. We call our children *Arrows*, and we call our adults *Bows*. See where I'm going with this? It's the responsibility of the Bow to propel the Arrow in an upward trajectory. (More on that later.) One of the most gratifying aspects of being an *Apostle of True Worship*, and Pastor of *"The Pre-eminent Church for The Teaching of True Worship"* (our church mantra) is that we are having such a profound impact on the lives of children and young adults. It is axiomatic that children are products of their environment, and that what a child sees, hears, and experiences during the first eight years of their life can add up to shape a child's development and can have lifelong effects. Children are born ready to learn, and they have many skills to learn over many years. They depend on parents, family members, and other caregivers as their first teachers to develop the right skills to become independent and lead healthy and successful lives. How the brain grows is strongly affected by the child's experiences with other people and the world.[55] I have witnessed firsthand the kind of trajectory shift that accompanies a child's growing up in an atmosphere of true Worship. The pictures you see here are of small children Worshiping at the altar of The New Olivet Worship Center in Memphis. Well, actually what they're doing is mimicking their parents and other adults. But isn't that how all learning takes place? Children do what they see, not what they're told.

Interestingly, and not surprisingly, what our Arrows (children) see Bows (adults) do, the Arrows imitate elsewhere. Such is the case with the six-year-old twin girls in this picture below. They constructed a comfortable makeshift altar, and told their mother, "Look Mommy, we're bowing like we do at chapel (which is what they call church)!"

The wonderful (and sometimes woeful) thing about children is that they eventually grow up! A child who learns how to Worship as a toddler develops into a Worshiping pre-adolescent, adolescent, and young adult. And if Worship has been inculcated into their way of living, they take Worship with them wherever they go, including to overseas destinations. Below is an image of one of our teenaged church members who traveled on a high school class trip to Quebec, Canada, where they visited the Basilica of Sainte-Anne-de-Beaupré, an important Catholic sanctuary situated along the banks of the Saint Lawrence River. In these photographs she is Worshiping. Strangely enough, my first experience with bowing publicly in church was during my second-grade school year at a Catholic school in Memphis called St. Augustine. Every morning during assembly we had to genuflect as we entered the sanctuary, then again when we got to our pew, then again as we left the pew to exit the sanctuary. As a child, I never thought it was weird or stupid. I just thought, "Hey, this is what they do, and I'm good with it." But kneeling at the altar was not something we typically saw in Black churches when we were growing up. As you can see in the images below, this young lady, whose peers were behind the camera, takes a very public stance by practicing two forms of Worship: prostration (on the left) and kneeling and blowing kisses (on the right). These photographs are courtesy of the young lady in them, Asiya Buchanan.

Another one of our teenage church members traveled overseas one summer and visited many revered tourist destinations. The following photographs are just a few of the ones she created. These photographs are courtesy of Ayante Williams. As you can see, Ayante Worshiped inside and/ or outside of iconic tourist attractions, including the Eiffel

Tower and Notre Dame Cathedral in Paris, France, and another majestic cathedral in Barcelona, Spain.

I hope you fully grasp the import of what the above photographs represent. In modern times, when peer pressure, bullying, public shaming, and even suicide surrounds young people's interactions with each other, it is virtually unheard of for a teenager like the one in the previous pictures to engage in such a highly moral public display of affection for God. The great news for the Body of Christ is that they are not the only ones!

"Worship is the most under-developed, under-researched, and unappreciated biblical concept in all of Christendom."

CHAPTER FOURTEEN

What Can We Expect After We Worship?

The following seven scriptural exegeses are actually adaptations of sermons I have preached over several months at The New Olivet Worship Center. I have included them here for a three-fold purpose:

1. To serve as a teaching/preaching guide for teachers/preachers who wish to explore the topic of Worship from a hermeneutical perspective.
2. To provide motivational reading for Christians and non-Christians alike who enjoy mental calisthenics toward fresh interpretations of scripture.
3. To inspire and motivate Worshipers to Worship with the expectation that something good will happen as a result of their Worship.

Please keep in mind, also, that these sermons are transcribed from audio recordings and thus reflect a more auditory character than that which is literary. They are also raw in the sense that they reflect my penchant for using slang, colloquialisms, innuendo, comedy, hyperbole, and anything else I think will reach the hearts and minds of listeners!

Worship's greatest value is that it consecrates our minds. What gives our life meaning is our faith in Jesus Christ. Without that continuous faith, we would have no moral compass at all. Our faith is what empowers us to keep moving forward. I'm not sure where I heard it first, but I have adopted the following acronym for faith: Forward Action In Trusting Him. The distinctive characteristic of faith is that it is always prospective. It always looks ahead and never backward. Our faith allows us to attack life each day with a never-give-up attitude. Worship plays an important role in feeding our faith. The question is what can we *expect* after we Worship? To expect means 3 things: (1) to regard something as likely to happen; (2) to believe that someone or something will arrive soon; (3) to look for something from someone as rightfully due under the circumstances.[56] Let's explore several texts with an eye toward mining spiritual nuggets or principles that can drive our Worship even when we don't feel like Worshiping. I'll call them "Worship Expectation" texts; "WE Text" for short!

WE Text Number 1. Matthew 8:1-4 (KJV).

1   *When he {Jesus} was come down from the mountain, great multitudes followed him.*

2   *And, behold, there came a leper and worshipped him, saying Lord, if thou wilt, thou canst make me clean.*

3   *And Jesus put forth his hand, and touched him, saying, I will; be thou clean. And immediately his leprosy was cleansed.*

4   And Jesus saith unto him, See thou tell no man; but go thy way, shew thyself to the priest, and offer the gift that Moses commanded, for a testimony unto them.

When he was come down from *what* mountain? The mountain on which he had just taught such life-altering concepts as: The Lord's Prayer, and the beatitudes, and how to fast with expectation, and "seek ye first the kingdom of God and his righteousness, and all these things shall be added unto you"...*that* mountain! And great multitudes followed him, because great multitudes always follow someone who they perceive as a benefit to their lives! Now, this is where we begin to get into what we can expect after we worship! Leprosy is defined as "an infectious disease that causes severe, disfiguring skin sores and nerve damage in the arms, legs, and skin areas around your body. Leprosy has been around since ancient times. Outbreaks have affected people on every continent."[57] Somebody's thinking, "Whew, I'm glad it won't affect me!" But there is what I call a spiritual leprosy that makes a person offensive, annoying, and infectious as well! This man didn't let his condition alter his decision to Worship Jesus. And remember, a great multitude was standing around. This man didn't let his witnesses alter his commitment to Worship Jesus. But he didn't just Worship Jesus and remain silent afterward. The verse says he Worshipped him, saying "Lord, if thou wilt, thou canst make me clean." He used his Worship as a prelude to a pronouncement. Notice, the man didn't pray a prayer, he made a pronouncement. He said to Jesus, "if you want to, you can make me clean." The word "clean" in the Greek means "free from being spoiled by sin and faults." It means "to purify from wickedness." It means "to be free from the guilt of sin."[58] It is clear from this text that this man, although he was a leper, still recognized his own sin. Sick people can be wicked too! Sick and wicked people can Worship too! You have no basis for expectation without Worship. And based on how Jesus reacted to this leper's Worship, I believe we can have some realistic expectations.

First, Jesus put forth his hand and touched him. As with most words in the scripture, especially New Testament scripture, the word *touch* has many nuances and layers as used in the original Greek translation. It means more than to literally touch someone with the hand or finger. It means "to fasten oneself to, adhere to, cling to."[59] *After we Worship, we can expect Jesus to touch us.* We can expect Jesus to "fasten" Himself to us, to adhere to us, to cling to us even in our spiritually leprous state, to latch on to us in our condition! And after Jesus touched the leper, he spoke to him. He said, "I will." In this context, the word "will" means "to have in mind; intend; to be resolved or determined; to purpose; to be fond of doing; to take delight in; to have pleasure in. It means "expressing a strong intention or assertion about the future."[60] *After we Worship, we can expect Jesus to say, "I WILL".* Jesus intends for us to be free, and after we Worship, we can expect his freeing touch. But Jesus didn't stop with a touch, he added a *word.* "Be thou clean." Not, "clean yourself up," or "go get somebody to clean you up." No, actually Jesus didn't tell this leper to do anything! He just told him to *be* clean. *After we Worship, we can expect Jesus' touch to empower us to simply be.* Finally, *after we Worship, we can expect to be given an assignment by Jesus.* There it is in verse 4: "And Jesus saith unto him, 'See thou tell no man; but go thy way, shew thyself to the priest, and offer the gift that Moses commanded, for a testimony unto them.'" I love the Message translation of the verse: **Jesus said,** *"Don't talk about this all over town. Just quietly present your healed body to the priest, along with the appropriate expressions of thanks to God.*

Your cleansed and grateful life, not your words, will bear witness to what I have done." After we Worship, we can expect Jesus to give us this assignment: Don't just talk the talk, walk the walk. But it's a very particular and detailed walk, a lifestyle with 3 components:

Component #1: Present your healed body to the priest. In other words, show up in the temple! Or, as my Grandma used to say, "Go to church!"

Component #2: Manifest the appropriate expressions of thanks to God. If you're reading this book, I don't have to explain to you what appropriate expressions of thanks are, but I will give you some examples. How about once you get to church, opening your mouth and thanking God by name? How about learning a lesson from any healthy toddler? When you give a toddler something they like, they will at least put a smile on their face. Once you get to church, how about a smile on your face every now and then? And if God has really been good to you, learn another lesson from my three year-old granddaughter. When we give her something she's just overjoyed about, she breaks into her "happy dance." Ain't no harm in getting your dance on at church if God has been *sho' nuff* good! (to quote my Grandma again!)

Component #3: Live a cleansed and grateful life. You don't live a cleansed and grateful life inside your head. It's not a "virtual" experience. It's a day-to-day walk in this world that identifies you as belonging to God.

WE Text Number 2. Matthew 8:1-4 (KJV).

My foundational premise for this series of messages is that there are several specific results we can expect after we Worship. And by "we," I mean all of us who take the time to Worship, including every mother under the sound of my voice. Today is all about you. {BTW, we've only begun to scratch the surface of Worship!} In addition, and I'm introducing this concept in today's sermon, there are also particular mindsets {mental pre-sets, I'll call them} that we can carry into our Worship that set the stage for those expectations. In other words, you don't just go into Worship with a drifting mindset. The devil wants us to drift in our minds. You know what it means to drift? Pre-set refers to something that is set in advance. To pre-set is to set or adjust a value that controls the operation of a device in advance of its use.

One of the mental presets that we can bring into our Worship is found in the first verse of our text, verse 18. Let's EXEGETE this text. Matthew 9:18-26 (KJV),

> *18   While he spake these things unto them, behold, there came a certain ruler, and worshipped him, saying, My daughter is even now dead: but come and lay thy hand upon her, and she shall live.*

The first mental pre-set you need going into Worship is that you be certain. I realize this may not be the sense in which most people would interpret this verse, but what did the man do after he's identified as "certain"? He Worshipped. And why did he Worship Jesus? Because he was certain of what Jesus could do! And look at what he was certain Jesus could do: Bring his daughter back to life. After we Worship, we can expect Jesus to bring life to a specific dead situation.

For this man, it was a dead daughter. What is it for you? What dead situation do you need resurrected? But that's not all we can expect after we Worship. Read on to verse 19,

> *19 And Jesus arose, and followed him, and so did his disciples.*

After we Worship, we can expect Jesus to arise and follow us, and we can expect some of his disciples to do the same!

> *20 And, behold, a woman, which was diseased with an issue of blood twelve years, came behind him, and touched the hem of his garment:*

After we Worship, we can expect sometimes a delay that seems like an interruption. Jesus was already on his way to the man's house, but here comes this woman, who was diseased with an issue of blood twelve years who steals the narrative! But just know that Jesus had not forgotten the certain man. God's delays are not interruptions; they're intermissions! And don't miss this: The woman with the issue of blood was a Worshiper too! Look at the verse again. How did she get to Jesus? She came behind and touched the hem of his garment. There is no way that this woman could have come from behind Jesus through a teeming throng of people without getting on her hands and knees and crawling. That, my friend, is Worship, especially when we hear her reason for approaching Jesus in the first place! Another mental pre-set is evident in the next verse.

> *21 For she said within herself, If I may but touch his garment, I shall be whole.*

Who was she talking to? Herself! On your way to Worship you need to give yourself a pep talk, a motivational talk. This wasn't about somebody else. This was about her. Sometimes it is about us. And that's okay. This woman Worshiped with expectation, and just as happened with the certain man, Jesus responded to this diseased woman. Look at verse 22.

22 But Jesus turned him about, and when he saw her, he said, Daughter, be of good comfort; thy faith hath made thee whole. And the woman was made whole from that hour.

Now this is the second time the word "whole" is used in the text, and I just don't think we can ignore it. The word whole means to rescue from danger or destruction; to be kept safe and sound; to make well, to heal, to restore to health; it means to save a suffering one from perishing.[61] And the verse says after she Worshiped, Jesus changed direction and spoke a word to her, but he didn't heal her! No, Jesus didn't heal the woman with the issue of blood. You don't believe it? Read the verse again: *Jesus turned him about, and when he saw her, he said, Daughter, be of good comfort; your faith has made you whole!* It was the woman's faith that healed her, not Jesus. After we Worship, we can expect a confirmation of the faith that led us to Worship in the first place! And she was made whole from that hour. From what hour? From the hour she Worshiped and submitted her body and mind to him.

Now, let's go back and check on the certain ruler. What did I tell you about God's delays earlier? God's delays are not interruptions; they're intermissions.

*23 And when Jesus came into the ruler's house, and saw
the minstrels and the people making a noise,*

Now, the word "minstrels" in the text means flute players or
musicians in the Greek text, but I'm going to exercise a bit of hermeneutical prerogative and update the reference to today's context
if you don't mind. The verse says Jesus came into the ruler's house
and saw the minstrels and the people making noise. I consider
myself a "fully functioning hermeneutical artist."[62] Hermeneutics
being the study of the methodological principles of interpretation (as of the Bible), or simply a method or principle of
interpretation.[63] My goal is always to show how biblical text
is relevant to current cultural contexts. My cultural context
as an African-American, I prefer the term Black, informs my
teaching and preaching. Our theology cannot be divorced
from our history as a people in the United States. That history has included a painful familiarity with the word "minstrel" that is used in this text. Minstrelsy or the minstrel show
was an American form of entertainment developed in the
early 19th century. The shows were performed by white people in make-up or blackface for the purpose of playing the
role of black people.[64] There were some Black minstrels as
well. Minstrel shows lampooned black people as dim-witted,
lazy, buffoonish, superstitious, and happy-go-lucky. After we
Worship, we can expect *spiritual* minstrels to try to minimize
and make fun of our Worship culture. Look at verse 24.

*24 He said unto them, Give place: for the maid is not
dead, but sleepeth. And they laughed him to scorn.*

Christianity's market share is shrinking. The percentage
of people who respect the Church and fear God is dwindling.

The world is not your friend. They are still laughing at Jesus. But not for long!

> *25 But when the people were put forth, he went in, and took her by the hand, and the maid arose.*

After we Worship, we can expect Jesus to evict the naysayers from our personal space, not our physical or geographical space, but our faith space. The verse says when the naysayers were put out, Jesus went in.

> *26 And the fame hereof went abroad into all that land.*

After we Worship, we can expect the fame of results of our faith to go abroad. Fame means the state of being known or talked about by many people, especially on account of notable achievements.[65] By faith, I'm claiming that as a result of your Worship many people will be impacted.

WE Text Number 3. Exodus 34:8-16

LORD, somebody listening to me right now doesn't feel wanted or needed. They don't feel like they belong. They don't feel important. They don't feel relevant… PLEASE use this sermon to. What is the mission of The New Olivet Worship Center? To be the preeminent church for the teaching of true Worship. There is more and more evidence lately that our mission is being carried out successfully. Look at this text I got from Deacon Olive Michael DeShazer yesterday afternoon. Worship's greatest value is that it consecrates the mind. I cannot overstate my absolute delight, real joy, and pleasure at having the opportunity to preach these messages on Worship to our college students, both recent graduates and those entering another year of matriculation in college or grad school, and high school graduates, and students, really all our children. Because you know what? It's about our children and our children's children. Not just mine, but all of ours. Let me show you who it's about. *ChandlerVideo*Delphine's grandkids. Let me say, parenthetically, that today, according to the Liturgical Calendar of the church universal, is referred to as Pentecost Sunday. Pentecost is celebrated on the seventh Sunday after Easter, and it commemorates the descent of the Holy Spirit upon the Apostles and other followers of Jesus Christ while they were in Jerusalem celebrating the Feast of Weeks, as described in the Acts of the Apostles (Acts 2:1–31). I mention Pentecost because if the Holy Ghost is already here, there are some things the Church should be accomplishing on a regular basis. I mean no disrespect with the observations I'm about to make, but if I am to be true to the mission of our church, these observations must be made. I will lift two recent civic/social/religion-inspired phenomena right here in Memphis. One is a 3-year-old coalition of faith-based, non-profit, and community groups called MICAH, which is an acronym for Memphis Interfaith Coalition for Action and Hope. The other is the so-called People's Convention that was held yesterday at what used to be known as Club Paradise {Where CANA Knight Bill Bolden and CANA Wife Doris Bolden were on a date one night several years before CANA when somebody got to shootin' and Bill and Doris hid under a table…}. MICAH, according to organizers, is calling for "equity" in Memphis, and they want to influence upcoming Memphis elections. Listen to what their Executive Director, who happens to be a preacher also, said when asked about that: "For us politics is, where is the power moving and is that power serving the people or holding them in place?" MICAH is "an organization of organizations", and that "The political process is helpful. It reminds us what tools we have as citizens," she said. "And one of those tools is access to and communication with and being open with our elected officials… But we have all kinds of other people power, spirit power and whether we come together around shared values even if we don't agree on everything." What in the world does that even mean?!?!? The People's Convention spokesman, also a preacher and Pastor, described the purpose of yesterday's event as "part of the Black civil rights movement and fight for Black liberation." He said he wants people to be able to vote on consensus candidates and said an even more important goal of the convention is to promote a progressive agenda. Again, what does that mean??? If Christians have embraced the Holy Ghost as Pentecost proves, why can't the church as it exists provide the leadership God's people need without forming nebulous, leaderless, quasi-religious social clubs? The question is "what can we expect after we Worship?" And today's text gives us some clear ideas, but let's get one thing straight before we go *anuhtha fuhtha*… One thing we can NOT expect is for God to do the work for us! Now, let's exegete this text. Exodus 34:8-16 (KJV)

> 8   And Moses made haste, and bowed his head toward the earth, and worshipped.

The defining characteristic of the texts I've been preaching in this "What Can We Expect After We Worship" series is that somebody in the text—I'll call them our protagonists—Worshiped! And the after-effects of their Worship, I believe, entitle us to certain expectations. In today's text, Exodus 34:8-16, it's Moses' turn. This was a dramatic time for the Israelites. You really ought to read the story for yourself sometime. They had just been delivered from Egypt, received the Ten Commandments of stone tablets, and *cut up* (another of my Grandmother's favorite sayings, meaning misbehaved!) so bad that Moses broke the stone tablets. And God had decided to give them a second chance! So according to the verse, Moses made haste, and bowed his head toward the earth, and worshipped. It's almost as if Moses wanted to hurry before God changed his mind! From this text I believe we see 7 expectations we can have after we Worship.

> 9   *And he said, If now I have found grace in thy sight, O Lord, let my Lord, I pray thee, go among us; for it is a stiffnecked people; and pardon our iniquity and our sin, and take us for thine inheritance.*

Expectation #1: We can expect to be in a good negotiating position with God. Moses is putting his personal reputation on the line with God. If I've found grace in your sight, Lord, go among us. That's an interesting phrase, isn't it? What does that mean, "go among us"? It means don't let us go by ourselves! {Lil Ken yesterday... His Daddy was featured at Curtis Givens' entertainment event on the grounds of Pink Palace Museum, sponsored by Moet Champagne, and he wanted to go.} And why did Moses want God to go? Because Israel was a "stiff-necked" people, that's why! Tell somebody, "Israel ain't the only one!" In other words, go among us, and pardon our sin and iniquity and our sin as we go, because I know us! Take us as your inheritance, God! To possess and enjoy, protect and defend, cultivate and improve, keep and preserve forever. Sounds like how 1st Lady feels about her jewelry, or Louis, Gucci, and Channel! You know what happened to Moses next??? God answered him! Ain't nothing like knowing God hears and answers.

Expectation #2: We can expect God to respond to our proposals. *10 And he said, Behold, I make a covenant: before all thy people I will do marvels, such as have not been done in all the earth, nor in any nation: and all the people among which thou art shall see the work of the Lord: for it is a terrible thing that I will do with thee.* Before I go on, I need to let us know: THESE ARE OUR PROMISES, Y'ALL! We are the seed of Abraham! By faith!

Which leads to…

Expectation #3: We can expect a beneficial alliance with God. COVENANT= treaty, alliance, league. MARVELS= signs, miracles, special displays of God's power, portents= a sign that something, especially something momentous, is likely to happen. TERRIBLE= that which will cause astonishment and awe; that which will inspire reverence or godly fear. And He says, "I'm going to do it *with* you!"

Expectation #4: We can expect to be held accountable by God to observe His commandments. *11 Observe thou that which I command thee this day: behold, I drive out before thee the Amorite, and the Canaanite, and the Hittite, and the Perizzite, and the Hivite, and the Jebusite.* I told you we can't expect God to do our work for us. And if we observe His commandments, He's gonna do His thing on our behalf! He'll drive out the Amorite, and the Canaanite, and the Hittite, and the Perizzite, and the Hivite, and the Jebusite. Now, those labels mean little to nothing to a 21st century Christian, but if you look at the original Hebrew meanings, I think you'll find encouragement. Look at the six groups God drove out of the land of promise, keeping in mind that the "land" where your promises are maintained is in your mind, or "faith space":

Amorite= "a sayer." You can expect God to drive out gossips from your faith space.

Canaanite= "Zealous." You can expect God to drive out those who have a "zeal of God, but not according to knowledge" from your faith space.

Hittite= "terror." You can expect God to drive out emotional terrorists from your faith space.

Perizzite= "belonging to a village." You can expect God to drive out people who are cowardly and are afraid to stand alone from your faith space.

Hivite= "villagers." You can expect God to drive out those who prey on Perizzites from your faith space.

Jebusite= "threshing place." You can expect God to drive out those whose sole intent is to separate you from your purpose from your faith space.

Only six nations are mentioned here, but there was a total of seven according to the biblical account. The seventh were the Girgashites. Why aren't the Girgashites mentioned here? Because as soon as they heard the Israelites were coming, they left of their own accord! Some people know that it doesn't pay to tangle with God's children! Either they left the land before the Israelites arrived, or they submitted to the Israelites as soon as they arrived. The name Girgashites literally means "dwelling on clayey soil". You see, they didn't have firm footing to begin with.

Expectation #6. We can expect a caveat from God concerning our personal behavior around the "inhabitants of the land" where we're going. *12 Take heed to thyself, lest thou make a covenant with the inhabitants of the land whither thou goest, lest it be for a snare in the midst of thee: 13 But ye shall destroy their altars, break their images, and cut down their groves:*

Expectation #6: We can expect clear instructions on offensive maneuvers once we attain our next breakthrough. *14 For thou shalt worship no other god: for the Lord, whose name is Jealous, is a jealous God: 15 Lest thou make a covenant with the inhabitants of the land, and they go a whoring after their gods, and do sacrifice unto their gods, and one call thee, and thou eat of his sacrifice;*

Expectation #7: We can expect God's rationale for delivering us to have something to do with our children! *16 And thou take of their daughters unto thy sons, and their daughters go a whoring after their gods, and make thy sons go a whoring after their gods.*

WE Text Number 4. Mark 5:15-20 (KJV).

15 And they come to Jesus, and see him that was possessed with the devil, and had the legion, sitting, and clothed, and in his right mind: and they were afraid.
16 And they that saw it told them how it befell to him that was possessed with the devil, and also concerning the swine.
17 And they began to pray him to depart out of their coasts.
18 And when he was come into the ship, he that had been possessed with the devil prayed him that he might be with him.
19 Howbeit Jesus suffered him not, but saith unto him, Go home to thy friends, and tell them how great things the Lord hath done for thee, and hath had compassion on thee.
20 And he departed, and began to publish in Decapolis how great things Jesus had done for him: and all men did marvel.

Worship's greatest value is that it consecrates the mind. The word consecrate is a verb, and it means to renew; to make perfect and complete; to add what is missing; to sanctify or set apart for God's use. Today, I do have another enumerated listing of possible expectations we can have after we Worship. It's still the story of a sick man. A sick man who received his deliverance because he, according to verse 6, "ran and worshipped Jesus" when he saw him afar off. Aside from the somewhat startling statistic that one in five Americans faces a mental health problem in any given year, the tricky thing about mental health issues is that many times, those of us who are having them don't even realize at the time that we're having a mental health issue! Therefore, absent a catastrophic event or some miraculous intervention, we go undiagnosed, untreated, and therefore unable to live the quality of life we would be able to live had we been diagnosed and treated. Not to mention the stigma, shame, and embarrassment society ignorantly places on mental illness. For the sake of review, here are the 5 most common misconceptions about mental illness:

Misconception #1: You're either mentally ill or mentally healthy.
Misconception #2: Mental illness is a sign of weakness.
Misconception #3: You can't prevent mental health problems.
Misconception #4: People with mental illness are violent.
Misconception #5: Mental health problems are forever {Not all mental health problems are curable. Schizophrenia, for example, doesn't go away. But most mental health problems are treatable.}[66]

And, here are some common mental health disorders among "us," as in Black Americans: (1)Major depression, (2) Attention deficit hyperactivity disorder, (3)suicide among young Black men, and (4)posttraumatic stress disorder due to the fact that Blacks are more likely to be victims of violent crime...perpetrated by other mentally ill Blacks.[67]

And before we exegete today's text let me add parenthetically that children can develop the same mental health conditions as adults, but their symptoms may be different. What is the same, though, is the result of Worship.

Now, let's exegete this text and see how many expectations we can have after we Worship under circumstances having to do with mental health issues! Mark 5:15-20 (KJV).

15 And they come to Jesus, and see him that was possessed with the devil, and had the legion, sitting, and clothed, and in his right mind: and they were afraid. Notice that after the sick man got delivered, he stayed close to Jesus. In verse 15, when the people came to Jesus they saw the man who had been possessed by the devil! To you it may be no big deal that the man was sitting, and clothed, and in his right mind. But if you had been that sick man it would be a big deal to you. Verse 5 tells us that before his encounter with Jesus the man was "always, night and day, in the mountains, and in the tombs, crying, and cutting himself with stones." He was a wild man with no peace and no comfort. And now, here he is at peace. Talk about peace. Somebody in here is on the verge of a breakdown because you have no peace. Sitting. And clothed, which suggests that he had been naked. And in his right mind, which suggests that he had been "in" his wrong mind! You won't admit it today, but somebody here today is in his or her wrong mind. Right mind means "sound mind"; able to exercise self-control; to think of one's self soberly; to be able to curb your passions. The inability to curb our passions indicates that we're "in" our wrong mind, and we need to get out of it. Take that mind off... My friend Donald Lawrence has a song with Dorinda Clark-Cole that says, "Let go of your natural thinking; embrace your righteous mind!" This man had embraced his righteous mind, and it had a ripple effect on the people around him, those who were used to him being "sick in the head." Here are some expectations you can have after you Worship and start thinking clearly and embrace your righteous mind. There are 7 of them.

16 And they that saw it told them how it befell to him that was possessed with the devil, and also concerning the swine. Expectation #1: After we Worship, we can expect witnesses to tell our story!

17 And they began to pray him to depart out of their coasts. Expectation #2: After we Worship, we can expect our peers to be confused and frightened by our deliverance.

18 And when he was come into the ship, he that had been possessed with the devil prayed him that he might be with him. Expectation #3: After we Worship, we can expect Jesus to willingly part company with anybody who doesn't want Him around. Expectation #4 is also found in verse 18. Expectation #4: After we Worship, we can expect to feel the need to get away from it all with Jesus!

19 Howbeit Jesus suffered him not, but saith unto him, Go home to thy friends, and tell them how great things the Lord hath done for thee, and hath had compassion on thee. Expectation #5: After we Worship, we can expect specific instructions from the Word of God. In this man's case, the instructions were to go home and witness to his friends. I think sometimes we underestimate the power of personal testimony. We talk to our friends about everything else, why not talk about what God has done?

20 And he departed, and began to publish in Decapolis how great things Jesus had done for him: and all men did marvel. Expectation #6: After we Worship, we can expect to become Jesus publishers (to proclaim openly something that has been done). Expectation #7 is also found in verse 20. Expectation #7: After we Worship, we can expect "all men to marvel" {be filled with wonder or astonishment}.

WE Text Number 5. Luke 7:36-50 (KJV).

36 When one of the Pharisees invited Jesus to have dinner with him, he went to the Pharisee's house and reclined at the table. PHARISEES= "separatist," literally "separated". A strong religious sect in 1ˢᵗ Century Palestine. They recognized in oral tradition a standard of belief and life. They sought for distinction and praise by outward observance of external rites and by outward forms of piety. There were no chairs at the table as we know them. Jesus had no reason to suspect that the man was trying to play him. We find out later that his name was Simon. *37 A woman in that town who lived a sinful life learned that Jesus was eating at the Pharisee's house, so she came there with an alabaster jar of perfume.* The woman "learned" that Jesus was eating at the Pharisee's house. Word gets around in a small town like Memphis... I mean Capernaum! Capernaum means "village of comfort," by the way. The verse doesn't say she *used* to live a sinful life. She was *presently* a sinner. And just so you know, we're not talking about a girl scout here. We're not even talking about an occasional backslider. Listen to what the word sinner means in Greek: It means, "devoted to sin"; "pre-eminently sinful"; "especially wicked"; "stained with certain definite vices." And let me just gon' and break that word "vices" down. It means in today's terms: "criminal activities involving prostitution, pornography, or drugs, due to a weakness of character." Okurrrr? And that's who crashed the Pharisee's dinner party! Annnnd furthermore... How in the H, E, double hockey sticks did she know where the Pharisee's house was? {At this point in the sermon I walked around the entire Sanctuary from front to back spraying a bottle of my wife's expensive Gucci perfume into the air above the congregants.} *38 As she stood behind him at his feet weeping, she began to wet his feet with her tears.*

Then she wiped them with her hair, kissed them and poured perfume on them. It takes a huge amount of weeping to produce tears that run down your cheeks, off your face, and onto something else to the point that the something else gets wet! The question is, what would make this pre-eminently sinful, especially wicked woman become so emotional?

The answer is, I DON'T KNOW. We're not told why. I don't know why. And, by the way, I think the word "why" might be the most useless word in the dictionary. What difference does it make, really? What matters is that her heartbreak was enough to open the floodgates. All we know is that this isn't a case of her eyes watering a little bit. In the words of Justin Timberlake, she "cried Jesus a river"! Now, we can engage is some speculation as to why. Maybe Jesus had broken her heart. And before you get on your self-righteous high horse, remember, Hebrews 4:15 says Jesus was "tempted in all points like as we are, yet without sin..." Maybe... Maybe... Maybe... She bathed His feet in her tears, and then...then she wiped His feet with her hair. Let's go back to our image of the extra-long Brazilian hair weave for a minute. {At this point in the sermon, I showed a Power Point slide picturing a woman, waist up from the rear, wearing a hair weave. I confessed in my introductory remarks at the outset of the sermon my ambivalence concerning women wearing hair weaves.} I think there's a lesson to be learned by me and everybody in this Sanctuary on this point. Bottom line: I don't think it matters what we do cosmetically to improve our appearance, or our self-esteem and self-image, as long as our new self-esteem and self-image leads to Jesus getting the glory out of our lives. And then she kissed His feet, and then she poured perfume on them. *39 When the Pharisee who had invited him saw this, he said to himself, "If this man were a prophet, he would know who is touching him and what kind of woman she is—that she is a sinner.*" I think each of us needs to ask ourselves this question: In what ways am I just like that Pharisee? *40 Jesus answered him, "Simon, I have something to tell you." "Tell me, teacher," he said.* Then Jesus took a left turn on him. Has the LORD ever taken a left turn on you? Jesus took a left turn and said, "Let me tell you a story!"

41 "Two people owed money to a certain moneylender. One owed him five hundred denarii, and the other fifty. If there's one thing this Pharisee understood, it was money. Here he was living in the lap of luxury. The name of his town was "Village of Comfort." He was very comfortable, so he knew how money worked. So Jesus hit him with what he knew best. Now, a denari is the equivalent of a day's pay. So, one man owed the moneylender 500 days' worth of pay. That's more than a year! And the other man owed him 50 days' worth. Meanwhile, remember now, this pre-eminently sinful woman is crying and drying, and wiping, and pouring!

42 Neither of them had the money to pay him back, so he forgave the debts of both. Now which of them will love him more? First of all, this is the kind of mindset I want to be able to have. To be able to forgive somebody's debt to me that's the equivalent of almost two years' worth of their salary! Neither of them had the money to pay him back, and he obviously didn't need the money {or maybe he did!}, so he forgave both of the debtors. Then Jesus asked the Pharisee, "Now, which of them will love the moneylender more?" *43 Simon replied, "I suppose the one who had the bigger debt forgiven." "You have judged correctly," Jesus said. 44 Then he turned toward the woman and said to Simon, "Do you see this woman? I came into your house. You did not give me any water for my feet, but she wet my feet with her tears and wiped them with her hair.* Jesus is such a smooth operator, ain't He? He turned to the woman, but he talked to Simon. Then He gave Simon a crash course in Christ-like hospitality. He juxtaposes Simon's *inaction* with the pre-eminently sinful woman's *action*. First, he asked him if he *saw* the woman. Sometimes, when we think we're above someone socially we don't even "see" them in public. You gave me no water for my feet. She wet my feet with her tears and wiped them with her hair. *45 You did not give me a kiss, but this woman, from the time I entered, has not stopped kissing my feet.* You gave me no kiss. We could talk about this for a while, huh? As a matter of fact, let's just put a pin right here and talk about the 800-pound gorilla in the room. The implication of Jesus' statement is that the man should, as a sign of hospitality, have kissed Jesus. Stay with me here. Romans 16:16 says, "Salute one another with a holy kiss."

1 Corinthians 16:20 says, "All the brethren greet you. Greet ye one another with an holy kiss."

I'm just readin'. Let's look at one more: John 13:23, "Now there was leaning on Jesus' bosom one of his disciples, whom Jesus loved." Grown men. And not just grown men dapping each other up, or giving high-fives, or slapping each other on the butt after hitting a homerun or draining a game-winning three-point shot. No, we're talking about grown men leaning on each other's bosoms. Anyway…[pregnant pause here]… Jesus told Simon "you gave me no kiss, but she' been kissing my feet since she got here, and she's still kissing them!" *46 You did not put oil on my head, but she has poured perfume on my feet.* You ain't poured no oil on my head! She don' po'd this expensive Gucci perfume on my feet! Then Jesus went on and resolved the issue:

47 Therefore, I tell you, her many sins have been forgiven—as her great love has shown. But whoever has been forgiven little loves little." Therefore. That's how you know it's being resolved. But y'all got to help me exegete this verse.

135

Read it: Her many sins have been forgiven, as her great love has shown. Wait, this is the first mention of love in the whole passage. In fact, the word love hasn't been mentioned so far in Luke 7 at all! So, in the words of Tina Turner, "What's love got to do with it? *48 Then Jesus said to her, "Your sins are forgiven."* Now, this next point is important. Jesus apparently didn't want the woman or Simon to be confused. In verse 47 he tells Simon, "Her sins have been forgiven…", but in verse 48 Jesus says to the woman, "Your sins are forgiven." And that's what started the buzz! *49 The other guests began to say among themselves, "Who is this who even forgives sins?"* The "other guests"…that's the crowd, ain't it? Who is this? But Jesus wasn't studn' the crowd. Jesus had a job to finish. He gave the pre-eminently sinful woman one more gift! Well, two more gifts! *50 Jesus said to the woman, "Your faith has saved you; go in peace."*

Anybody see what the two gifts were? Your faith has saved you. He gave her Salvation.

And He gave her a Benediction! Where are you in Simon's house? Are you Simon? Are you the pre-eminently sinful woman? Are you one of the "other guests?" Or…are you Jesus? Extending grace and favor to people who "don't deserve" it?

WE Text Number 6. Genesis 22:1-14 (KJV).

"What Can We Expect After We Worship? God Of All Or Not God At All Edition"
1 And it came to pass after these things, that God did tempt Abraham, and said unto him, Abraham: and he said, Behold, here I am.

After what things? After some "baby mama/baby daddy drama." Basically, after an Old Testament episode of "Real Housewives of Philistine"! In a nutshell, Abraham and Sarah had a son named Isaac when they were 100 years old, but Abraham had another son named Ishmael by his side chick, Hagar. And Sarah threw shade on Hagar and had Abraham put her and her son by Abraham out. And God told Abraham not to worry about it because He, God, was gon' make a great nation of Ishmael too. By the way, the Islamic Prophet Muhammad is believed to be a descendant of Ishmael! And just as a point of information, today Muslims around the world are celebrating a religious festival called Eid al-Adha to celebrate Abraham's sacrifices. So, anyway after God promised to take care of Hagar and Ishmael, Abraham entered into a covenant of peace with a military commander named Abimelech, and he built a well and called it Beersheba. Stay with me, I'm going somewhere with this. Then something very relevant to today's text happened. Look at the screen. Genesis 21, verses 33, the Message Bible:

33 Abraham planted a tamarisk tree in Beersheba and worshiped God there, praying to the Eternal God.

What can we expect after we Worship? Read verse 1 of our text again: "And it came to pass after these things, that God did tempt Abraham"! The word "tempt" here means to put to the test. I only have two expectations to tell you about today, and here's EXPECTATION #1: After we Worship, we can expect God to put us to the test. And there's only one question on the test. And the question is, "Are you in or not?" That's the question implicit in verse 2:

2 And he said, Take now thy son, thine only son Isaac, whom thou lovest, and get thee into the land of

*Moriah; and offer him there for a burnt offering upon
one of the mountains which I will tell thee of.*

Wait, wait, wait Pastor. Wait a minute! Did you not just
tell us that Abraham had another son named Ishmael? This,
then, appears to be a contradiction. By the way, the Bible
is filled with seeming contradictions, and I don't think we
can just ignore them. I think we have to deal with them on
a case-by-case basis. In this case, Isaac was Abraham's only
heir. God had approved of Sarah's decision to cut Ishmael
off from being Abraham's heir. He was no longer recognized
as Abraham's son. Don't act like you've never heard of a man
having children that nobody knew were his kids! God was
testing Abraham, and he was telling him, "I'm either God of
all, or I'm not God at all!"

*3 And Abraham rose up early in the morning, and saddled his
ass, and took two of his young men with him, and Isaac his son,
and clave the wood for the burnt offering, and rose up, and
went unto the place of which God had told him. 4 Then on the
third day Abraham lifted up his eyes, and saw the place afar off.*

Imagine this journey. It's a three-day journey, and every
day Abraham must be thinking about the fact that he gave
away one son and is about to kill the son he kept. Three
days he's second-guessing Sarah and probably missing Hagar.
I believe Abraham had feelings for Hagar. He may have loved
her. That's why they call the baby a "love child." Soul ties
go deep. Three days. And on the third day the text says he
looked up and saw the place afar off.

5 And Abraham said unto his young men, Abide
ye here with the ass; and I and the lad will go
yonder and worship, and come again to you.

Look at the faith manifested in Abraham's instructions
to his servants: Y'all stay here. Isaac and I are going over yonder to Worship, and we'll be back! Can you imagine having
that kind of faith? What does the word Worship mean here?
It's important to know exactly what he was about to do. Now,
we know that in the New Testament, the Greek word for
Worship is proskuneo, and the front inside cover of our bulletin tells us what it means in Greek: "to lay prostrate, bow,
kneel, and/or blow kisses to God in homage (special honor
shown publicly) and obeisance (a gesture expressing deferential respect.)" But our text today is not in the New Testament.
It's in the Old Testament. Could it be that the word Worship
means something different here than in the New Testament?
I suppose it could. And if it does, we're going to need to
re-examine our teachings on true Worship. You ready? Let's
go. The word Worship in the Hebrew here is spelled shâchâh,
pronounced "shahah," and it means…to bow down; to prostrate oneself before God in homage.

6 And Abraham took the wood of the burnt offering, and
laid it upon Isaac his son; and he took the fire in his hand,
and a knife; and they went both of them together. 7 And
Isaac spake unto Abraham his father, and said, My father:
and he said, Here am I, my son. And he said, Behold the fire
and the wood: but where is the lamb for a burnt offering?

Isaac had sense enough to know what's supposed to
happen at altars. Sacrifices happen at altars. Isaac knew that
whenever you go to the Altar, something is about to die. Did

you kill anything at the Altar today? And those were the last words that came out of Isaac's mouth. We don't hear from him again. All we know is that Abraham's answer must have satisfied Isaac, because look what happened in verse 8:

8 And Abraham said, My son, God will provide himself a lamb for a burnt offering: so, they went both of them together.

"Okay, Dad." That's what Isaac said by his actions, not with his lips. {At this point in the sermon, I demonstrated what the scene may have looked like, with a little boy holding my hand. Talk about what Abraham might have been thinking with every step...because the narrator doesn't tell us what Abraham is thinking...neither does it tell us what Isaac is thinking... He could have told us, but he didn't! So, we can use our imagination.}

9 And they came to the place which God had told him of; and Abraham built an altar there, and laid the wood in order, and bound Isaac his son, and laid him on the altar upon the wood.

"Shachah." He laid him on the altar upon the wood. I think it's important *how* he laid him on the wood.

*10 And Abraham stretched forth his hand,
and took the knife to slay his son.*

{Here I demonstrated how it may have looked as Abraham stretched for the knife...}

11 And the angel of the LORD called unto him out of heaven, and said, Abraham, Abraham: and he said, Here am I. 12 And he said, Lay not thine hand upon the lad, neither do thou anything unto him: for now I know that thou fearest God, seeing thou hast not withheld thy son, thine only son from me. 13 And Abraham lifted up his eyes, and looked, and behold behind him a ram caught in a thicket by his horns: and Abraham went and took the ram, and offered him up for a burnt offering in the stead of his son.

You mean to tell me Abraham was so focused on obeying God that he couldn't hear a whole ram "caught in a thicket"? He didn't hear the ram until he heard from God!

14 And Abraham called the name of that place Jehovah-jireh: as it is said to this day, In the mount of the LORD it shall be seen.

The name Jehovah-jireh means "the LORD will provide." Which brings us, finally, to EXPECTATION #2: After we Worship, we can expect the LORD to provide!

WE Text Number 7. John 4:6-30 (KJV).

Worship's greatest value is that it consecrates the mind. We need a consecrated mind, because a mind is a terrible thing to waste. The opposite of a consecrated mind is a de-consecrated, or desecrated mind.

DESECRATE= to treat with violent disrespect; violate; contaminate; adulterate; vitiate. Considering the great achievements our minds are capable of, a lot of us are guilty of desecrating our minds.

Mindset works both ways, positive and negative. We wouldn't be here if we weren't willing to accept and make certain assumptions. I confess that I have developed an obsession with regard to Worship. Obsessive people can be annoying.

I'm obsessed with Worship and scripture passages that talk about Worship. Case in point: Our scripture reading today is 25 verses! Our Sunday morning scripture readings are usually no more than 12 verses! My subject today is, "A Magnificent Obsession." An obsession is an idea or thought that continually preoccupies or intrudes on a person's mind. And the word "magnificent" speaks for itself. It means impressively beautiful, elaborate, or extravagant, striking, splendid, spectacular, glorious, superb, majestic, awesome, breathtaking, splendiferous, rare, splendacious, magnolious; sumptuous, resplendent, grand, imposing, monumental, palatial, noble, proud, stately, exalted, royal, regal, kingly, imperial, princely, opulent, fine, luxurious, lavish, rich, brilliant, radiant, dazzling, elegant, gorgeous, elevated, transcendent! Those are words I would use to describe my obsession with Worship! An obsession resembles an addiction, which is a habit, a craving, a compulsion. You ever heard a person refer to themselves, or be referred to as "OCD"? That's not usually a compliment! And in my case, I don't care whether it's a compliment or not. In fact, I don't care if it's the vilest of "put downs." OCD is an acronym that stands for Obsessive-Compulsive DISorder. Obsessive-compulsive disorder (OCD) is an anxiety disorder in which people have recurring, unwanted thoughts, ideas, or sensations (obsessions) that make them feel driven to do something repetitively (compulsions).

Now, let's exegete this text, and the text is so pregnant, I feel like I just want to read it and comment briefly behind each verse. But like I said, it's a lot of verses! So, if you don't mind, I'd like to begin at the end. And let me begin by saying, "Somebody in Samaria that day had a magnificent obsession!" How else can you explain one woman, an outcast at that, leading a city full of men to follow—wait for it—another man! Verse 28 says, "The woman then left her waterpot, and went her way into the city, and saith to the men." Verse 29 says she commanded them to "Come, see a man, which told me all things that ever I did." Then she asked them the following rhetorical question: "Is not this the Christ?" And verse 30 says, "Then they went out of the city, and came unto" Jesus! Now that's effective evangelism for yo' asterisk! And that's the end of the story. But how did we get there? I told you, we got there because somebody had a magnificent obsession! And I submit to you that everybody has one. In fact, it's my belief that everybody has at least one, which means some of us have more than one. The question for our purposes today is, Is Worship one of yours? Ask your neighbor, "Is Worship one of your magnificent obsessions?" I said earlier that it's my belief that everybody has at least one magnificent obsession. You don't believe me? Your Honor I'd like to submit Exhibit A, marked "Popeyes Chicken Sandwiches!" Our resident fried chicken expert, Reverend Ruby Johnson, informed me last night that last week Kroger was selling whole chickens for seventy-nine cents per pound. Look at the price of Popeyes Chicken Sandwich on that screen…(At this point in the sermon I showed a Power Point slide picturing a crowd of people standing in line waiting to purchase a Popeyes chicken sandwich for three dollars and ninety-nine cents. Then I remarked that people were willing to pay the price of five whole chickens for one chicken sandwich, which indicates an obsession with Popeyes chicken sandwiches!)

Okay, let's go back to the beginning now that we've started at the end.

6 Now Jacob's well was there. Jesus, therefore, being wearied with his journey, sat thus on the well: and it was about the sixth hour. The people of God are no strangers to wells. They dug a well every time God did something for them, or when they wanted God to do something for them! What if we did that? What would our front yards look like? What would our neighborhoods look like if we built a well every time God does something for us, or every time we wanted God to do something for us? "Jesus, therefore, being wearied of his journey," sat down on Jacob's well! Jesus got tired. I wonder if Jesus ever felt like singing, "Smile!... I ain't going back and forth wit' you...people!" *7 There cometh a woman of Samaria to draw water: Jesus saith unto her, Give me to drink.* Then this Samaritan woman came to the watering hole. You know that's what they used to call bars, right? {At this point I showed a Power Point slide picturing a man and woman casually drinking cocktails at a bar or pub.} And when she got there, Jesus asked her for a drink. That's not how it usually goes when we meet people in bars, is it? The man usually offers the woman a drink. He doesn't ask her for a drink. *8 (For his disciples were gone away unto the city to buy meat.)* Anybody notice the dichotomy here? Jesus asked for a *drink* when the disciples were gone to buy *meat.* Who was this woman? The text doesn't give us her name, so we don't know what to call her if we just deal with the "world of the text." But the "world behind the text" yields some intelligence we can use! Biblical scholarship has revealed that this woman is venerated as a Saint in Orthodox and Eastern Catholic traditions, and that her name is Photina, which means "luminous one." [LUMINOUS= full of or shedding light; bright or shining, especially in the dark.] Photina! That's a fascinating name to me. Anybody remember that song, "The Name Game"? Let's sing it using the name Photina!

Photina! Tina, Tina
Bo-bina, bo-na-na fanna
Fo-fina. fee fi mo-mina, Photina!

Anyway, Photina wasn't in the mood to just give Jesus a drink, apparently. At least not without striking up a conversation: *9 Then saith the woman of Samaria unto him, How is it that thou, being a Jew, askest drink of me, which am a woman of Samaria? for the Jews have no dealings with the Samaritans.* Photina clearly knew her "place," if you will. Meaning she knew where she stood with Jews and with men. Read it again. And it's clear she didn't like it, but apparently her feeling was, "It is what it is, until it ain't what it was." *10 Jesus answered and said unto her, If thou knewest the gift of God, and who it is that saith to thee, Give me to drink; thou wouldest have asked of him, and he would have given thee living water.* What was Jesus talking about when He said, "the gift of God"? Is Worship the gift He was talking about?

Was *he* the gift he was referring to? We don't really know for sure, y'all. All I do know is that Jesus wanted Photina to get to know him; again, that's what people who meet at watering holes usually want. *11 The woman saith unto him, Sir, thou hast nothing to draw with, and the well is deep: from whence then hast thou that living water?* Check out the flow of this conversation, y'all. This was an intimate conversation. Kind of like you'd have if you were meeting someone at a bar, and you weren't supposed to be at the bar with them. *12 Art thou greater than our father Jacob, which gave us the well, and drank thereof himself, and his children, and his cattle?* Some might say Photina was being sarcastic here, but I don't think so. I think she may have been genuinely impressed with Jesus' gravitas. And Jesus' answer was, in effect,

"Quite frankly, yes. I AM greater than your father Jacob!" *13 Jesus answered and said unto her, Whosoever drinketh of this water shall thirst again: 14 But whosoever drinketh of the water that I shall give him shall never thirst; but the water that I shall give him shall be in him a well of water spring-*

ing up into everlasting life. Mane, that's deep! Try to imagine water springing up, not just up, but up into something that is another form of itself! *15 The woman saith unto him, Sir, give me this water, that I thirst not, neither come hither to draw.* This verse speaks for itself. Photina wanted what Jesus had to offer. She said, "GIVE IT TO ME!" I'll let you decide how that particular reaction fits in to a scenario where an attractive woman and man meet and "hit it off" in a bar. *16 Jesus saith unto her, Go, call thy husband, and come hither.* My "fully functioning hermeneutical artist" interpretation of this verse is: "Oops." *17 The woman answered and said, I have no husband. Jesus said unto her, Thou hast well said, I have no husband: 18 For thou hast had five husbands; and he whom thou now hast is not thy husband: in that saidst thou truly. 19 The woman saith unto him, Sir, I perceive that thou art a prophet.* Photina had had five husbands. Big deal: Elizabeth Taylor had eight! And Dude she' sleeping with…playin' house with… ain't nunna huh huzzband…big deal. Isssa buuuuunch o' us that was livin' together as "friends with benefits" when we met Jesus! Or, as my Granddaddy used to say, "Tasting the milk before you buy the cow"! {Dear Reader: If you don't understand Black Ebonics, I suggest you Google the term, "Black Ebonics" 😊} Be that as it may! Or as Mother Jones used to say, "Howsunever"… Photina changed the subject real quick, okurr? *20 Our fathers worshipped in this mountain; and ye say, that in Jerusalem is the place where men ought to worship.* So, Photina says, "Bump all that, Jesus. I wanna talk about worship, because that's my magnificent obsession! That's what I've been searching for with all these husbands. That's what I'm searching for wit' Dude I'm shacking with right now. I might marry him, and I might not. And I might marry the next Dude I meet and fall in love with. And I ain't shamed! I'm trying to find the right one to give my body to as the ultimate act of love!" I'm trying to find the right one to give my body to as the ultimate act of love! I'm trying to find the right one to give my body to as the ultimate act of love! In essence, that's what worship really is; it's giving our bodies to God as the ultimate act of love. *21 Jesus saith unto her, Woman, believe me, the hour cometh, when ye shall neither in this mountain, nor yet at Jerusalem, worship the Father.* While we're searching, it's difficult to tell who we can believe. Here's Jesus telling Photina and telling us, "Believe *me*." Then He tells her why, and there's a sense of urgency in His voice: *22 Ye worship ye know not what: we know what we worship: for salvation is of the Jews. 23 But the hour cometh, and now is, when the true worshippers shall worship the Father in spirit and in truth: for the Father seeketh such to worship him. 24 God is a Spirit: and they that worship him must worship him in spirit and in truth.* This is a lot to unpack, but Photina didn't bother to unpack it, because she believed what Jesus said, and she already knew what Worship was. All she was missing was somebody to believe in! You can tell by what she says next: *25 The woman saith unto him, I know that Messias cometh, which is called Christ: when he is come, he will tell us all things. 26 Jesus saith unto her, I that speak unto thee am he.* That was all Photina needed to hear! Then, as is so often the case, right in the middle of her and Jesus really hitting it off...in the back, in the booth, in the corner, in the dark, if you will, yonder comes somebody who knows one of them! *27 And upon this came his disciples, and marvelled that he talked with the woman: yet no man said, What seekest thou? or, Why talkest thou with her? 28 The woman then left her waterpot, and went her way into the city, and saith to the men.* At this point, I can imagine the disciples reading the situation all wrong. Here dey go: "That's right! Get on outta here... Tramp! You know good and well we don't deal with your kind!" Photina obviously wasn't studdin them, despite what they may have thought. What was it that would make this streetwise woman abandon her pre-planned purpose, which was to simply get a pail of water to take back to her Dude at the house? What was it in Jesus' statement that would cause her to leave her water pot, the very instrumentation of her original intent, to go "her way," the verse says, into the city and recruit "the men"? Well, let's see what she says: *29 Come, see a man, which told me all things that ever I did: is not this the Christ?* This verse gives us insight into Photina's enthusiastic mindset. She was pumped about meeting Jesus! She was geeked about hooking up with "the Christ"! The word Christ here means "anointed," the anointed One and His anointing, the burden lifting, yoke destroying power and presence of almighty God. That's something to be excited about! Frangelica Rodgers prayed at KIRBS this week about being excited and thankful to be an Olive. She thanked the LORD for blessing her to be an Olive! You can be one too! But you have got to change positions! Maybe literally; maybe figuratively; maybe both. But do it today! The men of the city did. *30 Then they went out of the city, and came unto him.*

"Worship is the most under-developed, under-researched, and unappreciated biblical concept in all of Christendom."

ENDNOTES

1 Hip-Hop Is Not Our Enemy!, by Dr. Kenneth T. Whalum, Jr. can be purchased at www.amazon.com

2 You may purchase my booklet on fasting by emailing me at kwhalum@comcast.net

3 "Addict", Google, https://www.google.com/search?q=define%3A+addict

4 "Supplier", Google, https://www.google.com/search?q=definition+of+supplier

5 "Praise", https://www.studylight.org/lexicons/eng/hebrew/1984.html (Thayer's and Smith's Bible Dictionary.)

6 "Praise", Google, https://www.dictionary.com/browse/praise

7 Dr. Munroe was killed in a plane crash November 9, 2014. https://en.wikipedia.org/wiki/Myles_Munroe

8 The Purpose and Power of Love and Marriage, (Harrisburg, Pennsylvania: Destiny Image Publishers, Inc. 2012) pgs. 133,134.

9 "Worship", https://www.studylight.org/lexicons/eng/hebrew/7812.html (The Hebrew word is shachah, but because we're focusing on Jesus' New Testament words, we'll stick with the Greek translations.) (Thayer's and Smith's Bible Dictionary.)

10 "Worship", https://www.studylight.org/lexicons/eng/greek/4352.html (Thayer's and Smith's Bible Dictionary.)

11 "Reverence", Google, https://www.google.com/search?q=define%3A+reverence

12 "Prostration",Google,https://www.google.com/search?q=define%3A+prostration

13 "Homage", Google, https://www.google.com/search?q=define%3A+homage

14 "Obeisance", Google, https://www.google.com/search?q=define%3A+obeisance

15 "Deference", Google, https://www.google.com/search?q=define%3A+deference

16 "Humble", Google, https://www.google.com/search?q=define%3A+humble

17 "Humble", https://www.studylight.org/lexicons/eng/hebrew/3665.html

18 "Seeketh", https://www.studylight.org/lexicons/eng/greek/1567.html (Thayer's and Smith's Dictionary.)

19 "Jones", https://www.merriam-webster.com/dictionary/jones

20 "Worship", Google, https://www.google.com/search?q=define%3A+worship

21 "Parliament song lyrics", www.genius.com/Parliament

22 "What is FaceTime?", https://computer.howstuffworks.com/what-is-facetime.htm

23 "Prelude", https://www.google.com/search?q=define%3A+prelude

24 NBC News, www.instagram.com/nbcnews April 19, 2019.

25 "How Old Is Catholic Church?", https://www.bbc.co.uk/religion/religions/christianity/catholic/catholic_1.shtml

26 *Mitford M. Mathews, ed., A Dictionary of Americanisms on Historical Principles (Chicago, University of Chicago Press, 1951), I, pages 198-199.

27 https://web.cn.edu/kwheeler/documents/Letter_Birmingham_Jail

28 "King In The Wilderness", HBO Documentary.

29 "Tribute To A King: What is Worship?" https://www.facebook.com/100008637012234/videos/1849356462028903/

30 Listen to the entire sermon, https://www.americanrhetoric.com/speeches/mlkivebeentothemountaintop.htm

31 "Sick", Google, https://www.google.com/search?q=define%3A+sick

32 The Words of Martin Luther King, Jr., Martin Luther King, Jr. and Coretta Scott King (William Morrow Paperbacks, 2001), https://www.goodreads.com/book/show/773958.The_Words_of_Martin_Luther_King_Jr_

33 Martin Luther King, Jr. quote, www.azquotes.com

34 "Denial", https://pyramidfbh.com/what-are-the-stages-of-ptsd/

35 "Denial", https://www.merriam-webster.com/dictionary/denial

36 "Denial", www.meriam-webster/dictionary/denial

37 "White Supremacy", https://www.merriam-webster.com/dictionary/white%20supremacy

38 David Brooks, "The Case for Reparations", (New York Times March 7, 2019).

39 Ibid.
40 https://www.cnn.com/us/live-news/el-paso-dayton-shootings
41 "Christendom",https://www.google.com/search?q=define+christendom
42 "Christendom", www.wikipedia.org
43 "Christianity", https://www.google.com/search?q=define%3A+Christianity
44 Rodney J. Hunter, General Editor, Dictionary of Pastoral Care and Counseling (Nashville, Abingdon Press, 1990), 1339.
45 Donald K. McKim, Westminster Dictionary of Theological Terms (Westminster John Knox Press, Louisville, Kentucky), 307.
46 "Theory", https://www.google.com/search?q=define%3A+theory
47 Ibid.
48 Hebrews 11:1 King James Version
49 https://news.gallup.com/poll/341963/church-membership-falls-below-majority-first-time.aspx
50 https://lifewayresearch.com/?s=spiritual+but+not+religious
51 "Sanctify", www.studylight.org/lexicons/greek/sanctify
52 "Acknowledge", https://www.google.com/search?q=define%3A+acknowledge
53 "Process", https://www.google.com/search?q=define%3A+process
54 "Render", https://www.thefreedictionary.com/render
55 www.cdc.gov/ncbddd/childdevelopment/early-brain-development.html
56 "Expect", https://www.google.com/search?q=define%3A+expect
57 https://www.webmd.com/skin-problems-and-treatments/guide/leprosy-symptoms-treatments-history
58 "Clean", https://www.studylight.org/lexicons/eng/greek/2512
59 "Touch", https://www.studylight.org/lexicons/eng/greek/680.html
60 "Will", https://www.google.com/search?q=define%3A+will
61 "Whole", https://www.studylight.org/lexicons/eng/greek/5445
62 www.olivetbc.com
63 "Hermeneutic", www.merriam-webster.com/hermeneutic
64 For a visual image go to https://en.wikipedia.org/wiki/File:Minstrel_PosterBillyVanWare_edit.jpg
65 "Fame", www.merriam-webster.com/dictionary/fame
66 "Schizophrenia", https://www.psychologytoday.com/us/archive?search=schizophrenia
67 Common mental health disorders among African-Americans, www.nami.org (National Alliance on Mental Illness)